4/00

The
Perfect
Season

The Perfect Season

Why 1998 Was
Baseball's Greatest Year

TIM McCARVER
with Danny Peary

VILLARD BOOKS / New York

Library of Congress Cataloging-in-Publication Data

McCarver, Tim.
The perfect season : why 1998 was baseball's greatest year / Tim
McCarver with Danny Peary.
p.   cm.
ISBN 0-375-50330-7
1. Baseball—United States—History—20th century.   I. Peary,
Danny, 1949–   . II. Title.
GV863. A 1M22   1999
796.357'64'097309049—dc21   99-13423

Random House website address: www.atrandom.com

Printed in the United States of America on acid-free paper
Design by Meryl Sussman Levavi/digitext, inc.

24689753

First Edition

Acknowledgments

Danny Peary and I received much-needed help from a number of people during the conception, preparation, writing, and editing of this book. Foremost we thank our three friends who were there every step of the way: our agents, Robert L. Rosen and Jonathan Diamond, and our estimable editor, Ian Jackman, who never pressured us despite feeling pressure himself to get the book out in time for the 1999 baseball season.

We want to express our deep gratitude to Elinor Nauen, researcher extraordinaire.

And to Chris Tomasino and David Rosenthal, who established our connection with Random House.

At RLR Associates, Ltd., we also thank Craig Foster, Gary Rosen, Maury Gostfrand, Gail Lockhart, Gretchen Topping, Barbara Hadzicosmas, J. Lisa Dicker, Joe Iacono, and Tom Repicci.

At Villard/Random House we also thank: Ann Godoff, Adam Rothberg, Amy Edelman, Joanne Barracca, Daniel

Rembert, Tom Perry, James Lambert, Michael Burke, and Meryl Levavi. And we remember Wanda Chappell.

Finally, we recognize other individuals who helped us along the way: Steve Hirdt, Randi Roberts, Hillary Sweet, Edmund Berrigan, Sam Allison, Theresa Katz, Amy Jo Vegger, Jacqlyn Carpenter, Carol Hopkins, Cory and Norine Gann, Jeanie Dooha, Bob Nowacki, Suzanne Rafer, and Zoë Weaver.

We appreciate your contributions.

Contents

Introduction

The year 1998 wasn't just the greatest in baseball history; it was the greatest any sport has ever enjoyed. The remarkable home-run race in which both Mark McGwire and Sammy Sosa shattered Roger Maris's seasonal record and the New York Yankees' inexorable march to an amazing 125 victories and a world title were merely the marquee stories in a year of extraordinary achievements by individuals and teams. Rookie Kerry Wood struck out twenty batters in a game, David Wells tossed a perfect game, Barry Bonds became baseball's first 400 homer–400 stolen-base man, Cal Ripken ended his iron-man streak at 2,632 games, the Atlanta Braves had five 15-game winners, and on and on. It wasn't just that records fell or were equaled at an inordinate rate, but that so many were first established decades ago by such baseball immortals as Babe Ruth, Tris Speaker, Rogers Hornsby, and Hack Wilson and such fabled teams as the 1927 New York Yankees. While cheering the accomplishments of today's players and teams, fans got a free history lesson, gaining an appreciation of past players as well.

The home-run race certainly caught the attention of Americans with only a slight interest in baseball. To the television viewer, following the classy McGwire and Sosa was a welcome escape from watching the talking heads who debated about Clinton and the "Crisis in the White House" *ad nauseam*—a baseball star was preferable to a prosecuting Starr. Baseball also was a welcome respite for fans of other sports, because just as these two special men were showing everybody what was right about baseball, almost every other sport (basketball, football, boxing, swimming, even cycling, for heaven's sake) had its image tarnished by work stoppages, drug scandals, or ear-biting incidents.

However, I'm not one who believes that 1998 saved baseball. I think fans already had started to return in a big way because of an influx of exciting young talent, including shortstops Derek Jeter, Alex Rodriguez, and Nomar Garciaparra, and thrilling postseason play. When it turned out that the 1997 playoffs were on in the background while Linda Tripp and Monica Lewinsky engaged in their infamous phone conversations, then you knew baseball was back. There was no instant resurrection. What 1998 did was recapture the hearts of the most stubborn fans who had abandoned baseball after the 1994 strike and encourage passion for the grand old game to resurface. Significantly, for the first time in many years, baseball fans felt they were appreciated by the players and, in fact, had an impact on them. We saw that in ballparks across America, particularly during the postseason. The bond between fans and players, which once thrived but seemed to fade away as salaries escalated, was in some ways reestablished.

All was not golden during the 1998 season, on and off the field. The umpires were inconsistent; only high-salaried, large-market teams made the playoffs; self-serving owners continued to use hardball tactics to get cities to finance new ballparks; it wasn't until August that Bud Selig became the full-time commissioner; there was needless brouhaha over McGwire taking a legal, over-the-counter vitamin supplement; and so on. But no matter. The sport of baseball is characterized by imperfections—remember that *great* hitters make outs seven of ten times—so, ironically, a "perfect season" in baseball must include flaws and failures. What made 1998 so rewarding to fans, however, is that the players achieved so much as individuals and as a whole that the negatives virtually faded into the background. The flies in the ointment were killed off.

This volume is my remembrance of the year that even old-timers admit is the greatest baseball has ever experienced, the one year against which all future years will be compared. I begin the book with the season-long home-run chase of McGwire and Sosa and end with the Yankees' World Series victory. Between these two prominent pieces I include essays on what I think were the other major stories of the baseball season. As I move chronologically through the '98 season, I recount its most significant moments, the record-breaking achievements, and major events, including the World Series, that made the year unforgettable. However, since it's the human element that makes baseball so appealing, the focus of my essays, even those about postseason play, is on the individuals behind the accomplishments. (I also write about four deceased individuals who had profound impact on the year: Roger Maris, Dan Quisenberry, and broadcasters Richie Ashburn and Harry Caray.) From my standpoint—and I think fans will agree—what was amazing about this year of records is that such a high percentage of the game's reigning superstars and rising stars came through. It's almost as if they had a pact to do things in unison. Nobody wanted to be left out. This book is a tribute to these talented men and the perfect season they gave us.

—TIM MCCARVER
March 1999

The
Perfect
Season

Mark McGwire and Sammy Sosa

I wasn't a believer. I didn't think Mark McGwire, Sammy Sosa, or anyone else would break baseball's most glamorous record in 1998. In fact, I thought the microphone-waving reporters who doggedly trailed after McGwire during spring training on the basis of his 58 homers in 1997 were being irrational for thinking, even before the season began, that the Cardinals slugger had a legitimate shot at 62 home runs. Didn't they understand that his high home-run total in '97 wasn't an indicator that he would do it, but rather that he would not? Because, as I argued, no player could smash 120 homers over two years and average a Ruthian 60 homers—not even the Babe himself. (Who could fathom that after the 1998 season McGwire would have averaged 60 homers for *three* seasons?)

So I saw no good reason for the reporters' ranks to swell just because McGwire became the first St. Louis Cardinal to smash a grand slam on Opening Day and then matched Willie Mays's National League record by homering in the season's first four games. As did McGwire, I thought that the media was jumping the gun five months early, and setting him up to fail miserably and disappoint a lot of people. Constantly reminding reporters that he had to take it "one at-bat at a time," he soon got testy, complaining, "I don't know how anyone can get used to this—I'm sick of seeing my mug." I thought it was appropriate for the media to call attention to his hitting three homers in a game in both April and May; his 400th career homer on May 8, 128 at-bats quicker than Babe Ruth, who had been quickest to that milestone; and the two longest home runs in Busch Stadium history on the twelfth and sixteenth of May. But I didn't think the hype was legitimate. I had no idea that this was the beginning of what would be the six-month-long headline story for baseball's greatest season.

I remained skeptical into June, even as McGwire broke records for the fastest this and farthest that and the media hoopla increased. In past years, there had been a number of players who knocked balls out of ballparks at record clip early in the season—Ken Griffey, Jr., had almost made a habit of it—prompting newspaper editors and radio and television sports producers to dispatch scribes to the scene to get the scoop on the latest player to threaten Roger Maris. The media isn't supposed to be part of a story, but invariably the players' home-run outputs went down as the numbers of relentless reporters around them increased.

If you were a baseball fan in 1969, you remember the media frenzy surrounding young Reggie Jackson when he had a record thirty-seven homers at the All-Star break. Then you also recall how the reporters who hounded him and American League pitchers combined to hold him to just ten homers for the rest of the season. Potential challengers have been worn down by the media, wilted in the summer heat, or, as in the case of Matt Williams in the 1994 strike year, run into some roadblock that prevented them from making history. Since 1961, when Maris broke Babe Ruth's thirty-four-year-old record of sixty homers, an occasional batter passed fifty homers but no one made a serious late-September run at the record. In 1997, McGwire pounded twenty-four homers in just fifty-one games after the Cards acquired him from the Oakland A's on July 31, and he became the first player to hit his fifty-seventh and fifty-eighth homers while wearing a National League uniform— yet Maris's mark was never in jeopardy. I could envision McGwire reaching fifty home runs again in '98, but thought something would prevent him from going higher. Mark had a history of injuries, like the foot problems that cost him almost the entire 1993 and '94 seasons. Another possibility was that he would construct various psychological barriers. He might be consumed by the enormity of it all, or be so conscious of the anguish Maris experienced dealing with the press while chasing Ruth that he'd be discouraged from attempting something similar. There was also the chance that McGwire would have a long home-run drought, so from a mental or physical standpoint, it would be a superhuman feat. I just didn't think he could do it.

Then I changed my mind. I had to, because McGwire continued to homer with such frightening regularity and do it with such ease. And all the while he showed he had the mental toughness to stay focused on baseball despite scrutiny from the media that was so intense only Bill Clinton could have related to it. (In June he faced three times as many reporters each day as Maris did in September 1961.) At the All-Star break, McGwire's homer total stood at thirty-seven—which tied Jackson's record and was the most a Cardinal had hit for a full season in forty-nine years—and I now saw no reason why this six-foot-four Paul Bunyan couldn't muscle out twenty-five more homers by season's end.

Moreover, I believed two other players also had realistic chances to hit sixty-two home runs. Fresh off a fifty-six-homer season, 1997 American League MVP Ken Griffey, Jr., blasted thirty-five homers in Seattle's first eighty-five games. And then there was Sammy Sosa, who had thirty-three homers. The pride of the Chicago Cubs had come from nowhere. On the twenty-fourth of May, the thirty-year-old Dominican right fielder had only nine homers, compared to McGwire's twenty-four. But in June, Sosa busted out with a stunning twenty homers to break the major-league record of eighteen in a month that had been set by the Tigers' Rudy York in 1937. To get into the race to challenge a thirty-seven-year-old record, he smashed a sixty-one-year-old record. I already was saying he was more deserving than McGwire to be the eventual National League MVP because he was a much more versatile player and his surprising Cubs were well ahead of the disappointing Cardinals in the standings. It seems funny in ret-rospect, but I felt sincere regret that a shoulder injury kept Sosa from playing in a reserve role in the '98 All-Star Game because I felt only the Wrigley Field fans knew how good he was. I thought he missed a rare opportunity to show-case his talents to the entire country when most people still believed the Cubs had been foolish to give him one of baseball's richest contracts in 1997. I didn't predict that Sosa would soon grab everybody's attention and that his fame would spread like fire across a wheat field.

As the fans around the country became more excited, all three players picked up where they left off after the All-Star break. It had now become a full-fledged home-run race with plots and subplots. A fascinating theme: Almost every round-tripper meant something more to the individ-ual than just bringing him one step closer to Maris. There was always another story. For instance, when McGwire slugged his thirty-ninth and fortieth homers in a victory over visiting Houston on July 13, he moved past Billy Williams into twenty-third place on the all-time homer list with number 427 and passed Mickey Mantle and Harmon Killebrew into eighth place with his forty-seventh multi-homer game. When Griffey crushed his thirty-eighth and thirty-ninth homers against Texas on July 14, they not only pulled him to within one homer of McGwire but also were the 1,500th and 1,501st hits of his career at the age of twenty-eight. When McGwire slugged his forty-fourth homer against Colorado on July 26, he set the seasonal record for the St. Louis Cardinals, passing Johnny "Big Cat" Mize's record, which was set in 1940. The next day,

Sosa tied his career high with his fortieth homer to beat the hosting Arizona Diamondbacks 6–2. It was his second of the game and the first grand slam of his career after 246 homers, ending the longest string in major league history without a grand slam from the beginning of a career. Emphasizing that he had a touch for the dramatic in '98, Slammin' Sammy hit his career-high forty-first homer the next night in Arizona, and again it came with the bases loaded! On that same date, McGwire connected on his forty-fifth homer to break the record through July. Sosa would tie that record with *his* forty-fifth on the thirty-first.

At this point, I thought Griffey had the best shot of the three challengers at passing Maris because he had an uppercut swing, played in the Kingdome, and, more than his two rivals, was used to constant media attention. But in early August, McGwire and Sosa began to pull away and leave Griffey, contentedly, in their wake, unable to maintain the torrid pace. He would finish with an American League–leading fifty-six homers for the second consecutive year, yet, incredibly, still be fourteen homers behind the major-league leader and ten behind the runner-up! Like all the other players in baseball, Griffey would become just another fan as McGwire and Sosa moved on in what would be an epic two-man race. In fact, after McGwire broke the record, Griffey hired a plane to fly over Cinergy Field in Cincinnati (Griffey's hometown), where the Cardinals were playing, with a trailing banner that read CONGRATULATIONS!

Although Griffey was the one who benefited from playing half his games in an indoor stadium where weather is not a factor, it became increasingly clear that Sosa and McGwire were in the ideal parks for their home-run pursuits. Wrigley Field is not the home-run haven most fans assume it is, because when the winds blow in high flies will not carry into the stands. But Sosa has the ability to hit line drives with power from right-center to left-center, and at Wrigley those balls just shoot over the fence. He has the perfect home-run swing for that ballpark.

It's likely that McGwire would have set the home-run record in 1998 no matter what his home park was, because thirty-two of his blasts came on the road. However, it's obvious that in Busch Stadium, in front of an adoring crowd and sometimes his ten-year-old son, Matthew, who flew in from California to serve as batboy on occasion, McGwire was in a "zone." McGwire might have credited good "karma" for his ability to see ball, swing at ball, and send ball into orbit thirty-eight times during games and hundreds of other times during his well-attended batting practices at Busch. In 1967, I was on deck for the Cardinals when Orlando Cepeda crushed a down-and-in fastball down the left-field line two rows above the Stadium Club in the upper deck, and at the time I thought, "Man, maybe no one will ever hit a ball that far in this stadium again." Well, big Big Mac smoked six balls in batting practice that far every day. And during games, he hit balls as far as 545 feet (against Florida's Livan Hernandez). McGwire didn't just hit home runs; he made Busch Stadium look like a Little League park. He is the quintessential right-handed low-ball hitter and he has the right combination of power and lift to hit golf shots into the upper deck. I can imagine how his teammates felt watching this awesome display of power and hearing the fans ooh and ah every day. You talk about developing an inferiority complex. McGwire insisted he wasn't trying to hit home runs in '98 but he knew that if he so much as made contact, there was a very good chance the ball would leave the yard. In any case, he was the only player I have seen go through a whole season without getting cheated on his swing. Most power hitters have to start their swings early; and if the pitch is out of the strike zone, a checked-swing strike will result. Yet Mark was so locked-in mentally that he rarely checked his swing.

McGwire is a much more disciplined hitter than Sosa, and that contributes to his success. Last year, he was willing to walk 162 times, the second-highest total in history, rather than go outside the strike zone in an attempt to boost his homer total. Much more a student of hitting now than he was early in his career, McGwire realized that if he chased balls off the plate, that's all he would get. Because McGwire showed that he was willing to accept a walk, he forced pitchers to throw strikes if they intended to get him out—and when they came into his lair . . . bang! That he was patient enough to wait for good pitches and walk so much is remarkable considering the pressure of people expecting him to hit every pitch to Pluto.

I think Sosa was able to catch McGwire because he had this advantage over him: His main goal was to catch McGwire, while McGwire had to both go after Maris's record and look over his shoulder. Because he was rarely the frontrunner in the race, Sosa could concentrate solely on the home-run championship for 1998. Because of the media, McGwire had to worry about the past (Maris) and the present (Sosa), two home-run races. If McGwire succumbed to the pressures of chasing Maris, Sosa, hiding in ambush, would streak past him. But while Sosa certainly benefited from this circumstance, McGwire did too, because he was stimulated by Sosa to hit home runs. They fed off each other. For several days in August their battle was like a classic heavyweight fight in which the champion is reeling under the heavy blows of the challenger but repeatedly rallies and becomes the aggressor. Consider:

- On August 8, when the Cards hosted the Cubs, McGwire promptly ended his longest homerless drought of the season at 29 at-bats by hitting his 46th homer to pull three ahead of Sosa. However, Sosa tied the game in the ninth inning with his 44th homer.
- On August 10, Sosa finally caught McGwire by hitting his 45th and 46th homers against the Giants.
- A day later, on August 11, McGwire retook the home-run lead with his 47th homer against the Mets.
- On August 16, Sosa again tied McGwire by smashing his 47th homer against the Astros.
- On August 19, the Cubs hosted the Cards in a game for the ages. Sosa took over sole possession of the home-run lead for the first time with his 48th in the fifth inning. McGwire responded by hitting his 48th homer in the eighth inning to tie Sosa, and his 49th homer in the tenth to pass Sosa.

- On August 20, McGwire slugged two more homers in a twin bill against the Mets to move three ahead of Sosa with 51. (Sosa would catch him again at 54, 55, 62, 63, and 65 homers.)

It was obvious that McGwire didn't feel added pressure because of Sosa. Instead he was thrilled by the competition, glad to share the headlines with another slugger, and relieved that he and Sosa could share an experience that no one else in the world knew from the inside. McGwire has said that he decided on his own to become more cordial to the press beginning in August and to "just relax and enjoy the ride" rather than becoming angered by all the attention he was getting. But I'm sure he was influenced by the media-savvy Sosa, who was always cheery with reporters and winning new friends by blowing kisses at the camera. "Don't let them see you sweat" could have been Sammy's motto. Realizing the magnitude of his accomplishment, McGwire now seemed to have fun at press conferences, particularly the ones he held jointly with Sosa when their teams played.

In Sosa, McGwire found someone else who was motivated not by the chance for fortune and fame but by a love of baseball, and also the very real challenge to do something that had never been done and walk into history. I think it was Sosa who made McGwire realize that they could be ambassadors for the game. Sosa said, "I like the fact that baseball is touching [the fans] in their hearts." As America watched, a genuine bond of respect and affection formed between the white, "privileged" former USC student and the black, Spanish-speaking Sosa, who was so poor growing up in the Dominican Republic that he shined shoes, peddled oranges, and learned baseball while using rolled-up socks for a ball, a milk carton for a glove, and a tree limb for a bat. They are both decent men with big hearts: McGwire has a foundation to prevent child abuse, and after the season Sosa would collect an enormous amount of money for Hurricane Georges victims in the Dominican Republic.

In 1961, the press had made it out that when bosom buddies Roger Maris and Mickey Mantle were challenging Babe Ruth's record, there was anything but healthy competition because they were mortal enemies. That put a damper on the home-run race and made both men very uncomfortable, particularly Maris. But McGwire and Sosa would have none of that. They wouldn't dignify questions about their homer race having racial overtones and the notion that some fans were favoring one over the other based solely on skin color or heritage. They became each other's greatest champions. Sosa would tell reporters that McGwire would be the home-run king because "He's the man." While McGwire didn't say quite that, he did talk about Sosa's "unbelievable class" and remarked how he hoped they both passed Maris and shared the new record when the season ended. And this was all said with sincerity. America had rarely seen such sportsmanship, brotherhood, humility, and class wrapped in a competitive cocoon. This was both a baseball story and a human-interest story. McGwire and Sosa weren't only heroes as individuals but as a twosome. Two friendly heroes with alliterated names, no less. It was just amazing how many times in this two-month period their story could be found on the front pages of daily newspapers, including *The New York Times,* and as the lead story on news programs. McGwire and Sosa transcended sports, entered the national consciousness.

At the beginning of the year, McGwire told reporters that they shouldn't take him seriously as a challenger to Maris unless he reached fifty home runs before September 1. He did this on August 20, when he became the first major leaguer to hit at least fifty homers in three successive seasons. Now he was willing to concede to the press that he thought he could break the record because he always had productive Septembers. He stated it as fact, not worrying that he might be putting added pressure on himself. It is one thing to say you will do something and another to do it. McGwire was confident, although he had previously echoed Ted Williams: "There is nothing harder in all of sports than hitting a home run."

He resumed his pursuit, somehow managing to keep his nerves in check. "[His teammates] don't say anything more to him about home runs," said Cards pitcher Todd Stottlemyre, whom the Cards traded on July 31. "[They] can tell he doesn't want to talk about it, and nobody's going to question him because it's too damn big."

Playing in front of enormous crowds both at home and on the road, McGwire still made it look simple:

- His 52nd homer against Pittsburgh on August 22 gave him 162 for three years to break Babe Ruth's record.

- His 53rd homer against Pittsburgh on August 23 moved him into third place on the National League's single-season list.

- His 54th homer, a 509-foot blast against Florida on August 26, tied him with Ralph Kiner for the second most homers in a season in National League history.

- On August 30, on the same day Sosa hit his 54th homer against Houston to tie McGwire, McGwire broke the tie with his 55th homer, a 501-footer against Atlanta that established the record for most homers through August. (Sosa would tie this record the next day.)

- On September 1, a day after Sosa hit his 55th homer against the Reds to tie McGwire, McGwire slugged his 56th and 57th homers against the Marlins to break Hack Wilson's National League record of 56 homers, set in 1930.

- McGwire hit his 58th and 59th homers against the Marlins on September 2. He surpassed his own career high set in 1997, and tied Babe Ruth's 1921 mark for third place behind Roger Maris's 61 in 1961 and Ruth's 60 in 1927.

- On September 5, McGwire tied Ruth for second place with his 60th homer off the Reds' Dennis Reyes in a 7–0 home victory.

- As his father celebrated his 61st birthday on September 7 by sitting in the stands at Busch Stadium, McGwire lined his 61st homer into the left-field seats off the Cubs' Mike Morgan in a 3–2 victory. His father, the Maris family, and Sosa in right field applauded. (If it was a great coincidence that McGwire hit his 61st

homer on his father's 61st birthday, then it was downright eerie that on September 4, Sam Gordon, the
Sacramento restaurateur who purchased Roger Maris's
61st homer ball and donated it to Cooperstown, died
in his sleep at 91, two days before Maris's record fell.)

What I find most amazing about this flurry of home
runs by McGwire (besides that Sammy Sosa was hanging
right with him, with fifty-eight homers) is that people kept
coming out to the park to see him hit a homer and more
often than not he complied. It's like in those movies
where Babe Ruth or Lou Gehrig tells a boy in the hospital
that he'll homer for him that day and then goes out and
does it. McGwire hit homers as if he felt an obligation to
give the fans their money's worth by realizing their expectations.

On September 8, McGwire wanted to show his appreciation to the fans in St. Louis by homering on the last day
of the Cardinals' homestand, against Sammy Sosa and the
Chicago Cubs. The FOX network really hoped he would
come through once more because it had decided to tele-
vise the Tuesday-night game. It was a brave move because
FOX had done heavy promotion for the season opener of
King of the Hill and the debut of *Costello* and now were pre-
empting them on the chance that McGwire would hit his
record-breaker. You can imagine how relieved everyone at
FOX was when, in the fourth inning against Steve Trachsel,
McGwire hit a laser shot that might have gone through the
wall if it had been lower but just cleared it in left. Joe Buck,
my partner and play-by-play man, exclaimed, "You throw

this man a party every night, and he always delivers." McGwire even came through for a *network*.

McGwire was so stunned when the ball went over the fence that he missed first base and had to go back and tag it before rounding the bases, hugging first-base coach Dave McKay and Cubs along the way. The shot had traveled only 341 feet and, as Joe pointed out, "was his shortest homer of the year." Bob Brenly, our partner in the booth, didn't miss a beat when he said, "If you figure the distance between St. Louis and Cooperstown, it's his longest."

I don't think anyone will forget McGwire arriving at home plate and hugging everybody in a Cardinals uniform, after lifting his son, Matthew. It had an impact on viewers when this muscular giant of a man, who spent his off day on Thursday filming a promotional spot for his foundation, gave his young son a huge hug and kiss on national television. (He also touched a lot of people when he said, "Everything I do in life and in baseball now is for my son.") Emotional moment number two came when a happy Sosa ran in from right field and the two exchanged hugs. And then McGwire climbed into the stands to hug the Maris children, who had come to see him break their father's record. As he hugged them, he whispered, "Your father is in my heart." Throughout his journey to pass Maris, McGwire had always spoken with great respect for Maris's achievement, which he said had been harder than his own because for the most part the fans weren't supportive of Roger. Repeatedly, McGwire had told reporters that he wished he could speak to Maris to learn what he had been thinking in 1961. I'm sure that the Maris family appreciated that he made sure Roger's story was told along with his own.

McGwire's sixty-second homer fell between the fence and the stands, where it would be retrieved by a groundskeeper McGwire knew. Like many other friendly fans who might regret it later, he returned the ball to McGwire. By this time, in both St. Louis and Chicago, any fan who didn't return the ball to McGwire or Sosa was worse than a serial killer, political assassin, and international drug dealer rolled into one. The lowest of the low. McGwire gave away almost everything to Cooperstown, family, and friends.

After McGwire hit his record-breaking homer, I thought he'd either relax so much he'd go on a home-run tear or relax too much and let Sammy Sosa whiz past him. In fact, Sosa again caught up to McGwire on the thirteenth, when he also passed Maris with his sixty-second homer. Naturally, that's when McGwire got his second wind and they both started hitting the longball. After McGwire hit his sixty-third homer on September 15, Sosa tied him on September 16. McGwire hit his sixty-fourth homer on September 18 and sixty-fifth on September 20, but Sosa tied him on the twenty-third by going deep twice. It was amazing how they responded to each other.

As much as I admire Sosa, I thought that it would have been a shame if McGwire didn't win the home-run race. After all he had been through, it would have been unfair if he finished second to Sosa, because fans might forget he was the one who had broken the record in the first place.

He also had been burdened by immense media pressure all year long, unlike Sosa. I still thought Sosa should be voted the MVP but I thought the homer title should go to the legitimate slugger who had been building up to the record in the last two years, not to the aberration.

Sammy Sosa became the first player ever to hit sixty-six homers in the major leagues. That number, that record, is part of his legacy. It was probably fated that he remain at sixty-six homers for the rest of the season because in that way his name will always be linked to the record he held. Also: *SS66* would look cool on a vanity license-plate. Sosa held the record by himself for all of forty-five minutes. At Busch Stadium, McGwire blasted his sixty-sixth home run off the Expos' Shayne Bennett in a 6–5 victory. The next day he built on his legend by slugging his sixty-seventh and sixty-eighth homers against the Expos' Dustin Hermanson and Kirk Bullinger. Then on September 27, the final day of the season, McGwire did the impossible by hitting two more homers off the Expos' Mike Thurman and Carl Pavano. The one off Pavano traveled exactly 370 feet, which was appropriate because it was his seventieth home run! As it went over the fence the $9 ball's value suddenly rose to $2.7 million. Although mentally and physically exhausted, McGwire had slammed five homers in three games to beat out Sosa in the greatest home-run race of all time and establish the new single-season home-run record.

If you look at their career statistics, the two numbers jump out at you: 70 and 66! They're located at the bottom of their seasonal home-run columns, below much smaller numbers. Nobody in major-league history has home-run numbers that high. 70 and 66? They look like typos or misprints. But you know they are correct because you were there when Mark McGwire and Sammy Sosa both passed and then obliterated Roger Maris's record of sixty-one homers set in '61. Yet, these months later, you still shake your head in disbelief as you look at those two mind-boggling stats. Seventy home runs for McGwire, sixty-six home runs for Sosa. In the same season, 1998.

Richie Ashburn

ASHBURN: Where were you this morning?

McCARVER: I had to go to a funeral.

ASHBURN: Was there an open casket?

McCARVER: At the wake last night, yeah.

ASHBURN: Do you know why I think there should be open caskets?

McCARVER: Why?

ASHBURN: Because most people show up just to make sure the son of a bitch is dead.

When the Philadelphia Phillies opened the 1998 season, it was the first time since 1963 that Richie Ashburn was not up in the booth delivering his classic lines. At the age of seventy, Ashburn had died of cardiac arrest on September 9, 1997. It was only hours after he had called his last game and a few weeks before he would have completed his thirty-fifth year as a Phillies broadcaster. I'm sure he would have been pleased that I smiled at his viewing when I saw that he had a closed casket. Since I had spent most of the seventies with the Phillies while Ashburn was at the microphone and then spent my first three years as a broadcaster working Phillies games with him (and Harry Kalas, Andy Muster, and Chris Wheeler), I could never imagine a time when he wouldn't be delivering his relaxed, funny color commentary for the team he once starred on. No doubt it was extremely difficult for Phillies fans last year to adjust to life without the most revered sports figure in the history of Philadelphia. So deep in mourning were the fans that the whole city stopped for two days.

Whitey, as everyone called him, was elected to the Hall of Fame in 1995, and I'm glad it happened while he was alive and could enjoy the honor. It was a crime that he had to wait so long, because he had a brilliant career, albeit overshadowed by the three slugging center fielders in New York during the fifties. I think it should have been Willie, Mickey, Whitey, and the Duke. Whitey was a superb leadoff man and center fielder for the Phillies from 1948 to 1959, before spending two seasons with the Cubs, and his final year with the 1962 Mets. He batted over .300 eight times, including a .306 average with those 40-120 Mets that, much to his consternation, resulted in the indignity of being selected the MVP for the worst team in baseball history. (Not surprisingly, the boat he received from Mets management sank on its maiden voyage on a lake near Tilden, Nebraska.) He won two NL batting titles and just missed capturing two more. Three times he had over 200 hits to lead the league and no one had more than his 1,875 hits from 1950 to 1959. A contact hitter, he'd choke up on the bat and slap seeing-eye liners over the infield and into the gaps. When he wanted a walk, his strategy was to keep fouling off two-strike pitches until he walked. "Pitchers called him a pest—some called him worse," laughed his Phillies catcher Stan Lopata. "I think the owners did, too, because he hit so many foul balls in the stands that it cost them money." He was such a good foul-ball hitter that once when a heckler in the fifth row behind the dugout was riding a teammate, Ashburn hit him in the chest with a laser shot. However, Ashburn claimed it wasn't intentional when he struck the same female fan twice, the second time while she was being carried out on a stretcher.

Ashburn was a superb base runner who had the speed to twice lead the league in triples and to swipe 234 bases in an era when stolen bases were not in vogue. He joked that he first realized he had inordinate speed when he was a boy and could chase down rabbits in the Nebraska cornfields. I believed him about the rabbits, but not when he swore to me that when he was a star running back in high school, he was *never* tackled.

Interestingly, Ashburn started his professional career as a catcher (for two years in Utica, New York), but was switched to the outfield once everyone noticed that whenever he had to back up first, he outraced every batter down the baseline. It was his speed and instincts that would help Ashburn record six of the top ten all-time seasonal putout marks for outfielders. Not even Willie Mays chased down more flies than Ashburn.

Although Whitey didn't possess a strong arm, his most famous play was the throw that easily nailed Cal Abrams at the plate on a single by Duke Snider to prevent Brooklyn from winning the final game of the 1950 season, which would have forced a play-off with the Phillies. It happened in the bottom of the ninth inning, a half-inning before Dick Sisler's three-run homer clinched the pennant for the Whiz Kids. Both Snider and Dodgers third-base coach Wes Stock, who sent Abrams from second with nobody out, couldn't believe that Ashburn was playing so shallow against the Dodgers slugger that he could make the play.

When Ashburn finally retired from baseball at the age of thirty-five, he still had an insatiable appetite for competition, so he took up racquet sports. Despite his advanced age he became one of the top five squash players in the country. He also became a tennis player nonpareil. When he was in his late sixties he was still beating Phillies players at tennis. A frustrated Lenny Dykstra once grumbled, "That dude might be old, but he gets to every ball." (He used to beat Lenny like a bongo.)

Whitey also played golf, but his score suffered because he was the worst putter in the world. He loved to stand over a putt with a cigar hanging out of his mouth, and talk. He'd say, "Boys, if you think this is pressure, think about the pressure of winning a batting title. I've had this putt a thousand times." And he'd putt confidently, and invariably the ball would go to the left or right of the cup.

A horrible putt. And he'd fume, "Jesus Christ, how can I miss a three-foot putt?" Or he'd curse, "Hog piss!" And we'd ask, "Hog piss?" There was a lot of Nebraska in that remark.

Whitey almost returned to Nebraska to run for office when his baseball career ended, but he accepted an offer to return to Philadelphia as a broadcaster. He was a natural—honest, affable, and possessing a biting dry wit. The central point of his minimalist philosophy was "If you don't have anything to say, don't say it," which he seemed to have concocted just to tell me. After Whitey's death, Terry Bitman, writing in *The Philadelphia Inquirer,* accurately summarized his personality as an analyst and occasional play-by-play man:

> Richie Ashburn was the Will Rogers of Philadelphia sports broadcasting—droll, homespun, opinionated and self-deprecating. Whether he was talking about playing for the woeful '62 Mets . . . , wishing a happy birthday to a 90-year-old fan, thanking people for the cookies they had sent to the booth, or describing a potential base-stealer as looking "runnerish," Phillies fans never tired of listening to the pipe-smoking man in the colorful cap, the man with the Midwestern drawl as soft and plain as a stalk of wheat.

Oh, yeah, "the pipe-smoking man." When I started working with Whitey in 1980, I noticed that he would clean and put tobacco in his pipe while he was doing play-by-play, not just when he was doing color. It was hilarious because listeners would hear the tap, tap, tap while he was describing the scene. He would also eat peanuts during play-by-play. So they would hear, "Ground ball to ... *crunch, crunch* ... short." And when Whitey opened his mail on the air, they'd hear play-by-play announcer Harry Kalas say, "There's a fly to shallow left field for an easy out," and in the background, Whitey would yell, "Hey, I already paid this bill!"

As a play-by-play man, Whitey always enjoyed putting me on the spot, especially since I was new to the business. He'd be complaining about an umpire's call and he'd turn to me and say, "You're the analyst, what do you think? Say something. Support me!" So I'd say something like, "You know, sometimes a pitch can go either way." And he'd come up with something entirely out of the blue like, "When you think about it, you've probably spent more time with umpires than you have with your wife." My jaw would drop and I'd ask myself, "Where is he going with this?"

Another time, Whitey's scorecard blew away so I let him look at mine. But every time he'd look at my score-keeping to find out what a particular hitter did in his earlier at-bats, he'd snap at me, "What does this mean?" After several batters, he fessed up to the audience and said, "I gotta tell you I lost my scorecard and I'm trying to read McCarver's, but he's got the worst penmanship I've ever seen." And he kept this up and I was roaring with laughter. For weeks afterward fans were writing in to tell us, "Boy, that was a great act." Act? That was just Whitey.

I had been in the booth only two months when I started talking on the air to Whitey about how injured

Phillies pitcher Larry Christenson had stopped by Mount Saint Helens in his home state of Washington and had brought back two sacks of volcanic ash from the recent eruption. I said that I'd looked at the ash and had discovered that there were two kinds. There was a fine, silklike ash from the explosive side of the mountain and a coarse ash from the less explosive side. After allowing me to finish, Whitey said, "I thought if you've seen one piece of ash, you've seen them all." I froze. Eight seconds of nothing on the air. I thought my career was over. I wanted to just pretend nothing had happened. But after a ball was fouled back, Whitey added, "You know, you're going to get us both run out of town." Now he was shifting the blame to me! For the next two weeks the local papers alluded to what Whitey had said. Were they out for his head? Nah, they just chalked it up as one more of the great clever remarks he'd improvised during his broadcasting career.

If it had been anybody else but Richie Ashburn, he would have been thrown off the air. But not Whitey. He was so beloved that he could have said anything and it would have been taken in the best way. So that's why from then on whenever I worked with him I just sat back, relaxed, and enjoyed him. I just enjoyed him. I felt lucky to be in his presence as I learned the tools of broadcasting, because I realized what the Phillie fans already knew: that Richie Ashburn was one of life's treasures.

Harry Caray

If he had been there in body, Harry Caray would have rejoiced in the great season the Chicago Cubs had in 1998, with the heroics of Sammy Sosa, the emergence of rookie Kerry Wood, and the Cubs reaching the play-offs. At least Harry, who died on February 18, was there in spirit at every home game, as everyone who came to Wrigley Field would attest. Nobody with such a strong personality who made such an impact on the game and on his profession would leave immediately—he had to be grandfathered out, in a sense. Those who cherished his memory felt it easier to sense Harry's presence at Wrigley because his grandson Chip Caray served his first year as a Cubs broadcaster in 1998. And for the April 3 home opener, his wife, Dutchie, carried on Harry's tradition by singing "Take Me

Out to the Ball Game" during the seventh-inning stretch as the fans sang along. Dutchie was the first in a year-long parade of celebrity and sports stand-ins, many of whom didn't know the words and whose voices (Mike Ditka is no singer!) would be illegal in forty-nine states. Harry really did believe the lyrics to the song. You could just hear baseball's greatest salesman saying in that trademark craggy voice, "You can't beat fun at the old ballpark." That's why the six months of fun at Wrigley Field in 1998 was the ideal tribute to the man who had been Chicago's second-most popular figure.

Harry shook so many hands and signed so many autographs that I think half of America knew him personally. I felt I knew him even before I met him because as a boy in Memphis I loved hearing his St. Louis Cardinals radio broadcasts over KMOX. All of us kids would pretend to be various ballplayers when we played in the sandlots and backyards, but there was only one broadcaster we'd ever mimic. So when we played, the "voice" of Harry Caray was always describing the action, even if delivered by high-pitched eleven-year-olds. His narration made our games official.

When I signed with the Cardinals in 1959, and was driven to St. Louis to work out with the team, I realized that there was a great possibility that I'd meet this legendary figure. After all, Harry ruled the town and was going to make sure that he greeted anyone who showed up. Sure enough, on the second day, Harry took me over to the television studios to interview me. I was scared to death. Years later, Harry recalled, "There was this brash seventeen-year-old kid, who would say 'yes, sir,' and 'no, sir,' and he couldn't have been a nicer young man, and now today he's a broadcaster of national notoriety! I don't believe it. Only in America!" That was his shtick with me till the very end.

When I first met Harry it was surreal because he sounded just like he did on the radio. I'd tell my friends back in Memphis, "You know, he actually talks like that!" (As Michael Hirsle and Mitch Martin would write in the *Chicago Tribune,* "Caray's voice was unmistakable. Fingernails on chalkboard to some, as calming as the sound of the ocean to others, the sound of baseball to all.")

Fortunately, when I did that first interview with Harry I didn't automatically do my "Harry Caray" in response to the real thing, although I remember the temptation. However, sometime in the 1980s, during a rain delay at Wrigley Field, he was on the air, and to fill time he said to me, "McCarver, I understand you do a great impersonation of me." I laughed. "Well, Harry, everybody does a great impersonation of you." He asked, "Do you want to do it for me now?" Harry liked my impersonation, but he got a bigger kick out of Bob Uecker's. Harry raved, "Bob, you sound just like me on the air!"

As I learned, Harry's entire on-air persona was like his real-life persona. He had the same boundless energy that he'd put into a radio broadcast. He really was a bigger-than-life person who was comfortable enough to—and I cringe when I think about it—wear Bermuda shorts to spring training. He'd be standing there among the professional athletes wearing those shorts and exhibiting the world's ugliest legs. He had a big frame from his knees up but then he had these needly calves and ankles. Everyone used to kid about those legs, but not to Harry's face. Nobody was man enough to do that.

Harry had such a common-man quality in his broadcasts that everyone believed everything he said. He claimed that the St. Louis sportswriters became so jealous that fans considered him to be the authority that they deliberately stopped putting his name in their columns. It was akin to censorship. You know Harry hated this treatment because in later years he would crave publicity so much that he'd deliberately mangle players' names just to get a mention in the papers. (Years later there was word that Michael Jordan refused to be interviewed by Harry because he feared being referred to as Michael Jackson.) Nonetheless, Harry maintained his lofty position with the public. One way he did so was to mention the fans right on the air. He'd say, "Ed and Martha Pritchard are here from Ames, Iowa," or "I'd like to welcome the Monroe family from Lawrence, Kansas." He would continue this practice to the end. In fact, his Cubs broadcast partner Steve Stone told me how people would line up to give Harry their names. Harry would come into the booth with a long list and would randomly rattle some off during the game. "That's strike one," he'd say, "and I want to mention that Charlie and Marie Stoddard are here today from Dubuque. There's strike two." By the time a half inning had gone by, he'd welcomed ten couples from ten different towns. So the common people loved him. And so did the celebrities who could hear him. For instance, Elvis Presley was a huge fan. (Probably Harry told the story of meeting Elvis for the first time more than any of his oft-told tales.)

Phil Rizzuto became famous for mentioning fans' names while broadcasting Yankee games, but Harry did it way before him—just as he used the catchphrase "Holy Cow!" long before Rizzuto adopted it. And before Rizzuto, Harry started plugging restaurants that he frequented at home and on the road. Likewise, this practice continued through the decades. As an example, in the seventies he might tell his listeners, "Well, let's see, Tim McCarver is still with the Phillies. They're in Chicago tonight, and knowing McCarver, he's probably dining tonight at Gino and Georgetti's. Probably got one of those sixteen-ounce steaks in front of him as we speak." He might go on to mention another five restaurants, knowing he'd get superior service whenever he'd turn up there.

Harry liked to live life to the fullest, and naturally that meant he had his vices, including smoking cigarettes, drinking liquor, and playing cards. Harry's game was gin rummy, and he'd play all night while smoking and downing martinis. He'd play with Gussie Busch, the owner of the Cards, and his broadcast partner Buddy Blatner, and whoever else could stand his wonderfully tacky antics. He became notorious for looking at his cards and—everybody knew it was coming—asking, "Hey, what do you make a martini with? . . . Gin!" And a few minutes later, "Hey, again! Gin again! I don't believe it!" Not only did he take your money but he'd gloat and rub your nose in it.

In 1968 Harry was in a horrible accident—he was run over by a car and had his legs broken. The Cardinals were over in Japan at the time, but it would be less than honest of me to say that everybody was sad about it. In the sixties, there were few players on the team who got along with Harry. Too often Harry got away with denigrating Cards players. He had become so powerful that no one would refute him. He was like Judge Roy Bean—if he didn't like you, he'd hang you. For instance, early in the sixties, Kenny Boyer begged off doing a radio interview with Harry because he had to play a twi-night doubleheader and a day game the next day. They'd gotten along until that time, but suddenly Harry threatened, "Do you know I can make you or break you with my microphone?" And Kenny, who took no guff from anyone, said, "You can stick that mike right up your ass." From that day on, Harry would say on the air, "Eddie Mathews is the best third baseman in the National League. Look at that range—do you think Boyer could make that play? No way!" Or "Great backhand by Mathews" and "Routine play by Boyer." Kenny was so revered by his teammates, who would call him Captain long after he retired, that this incident further strained relations between the players and Harry.

Caray's long broadcasting career with the Cardinals ended prior to the 1970 season. How popular had he been in St. Louis? Move ahead fifteen years to 1985, when Jack Buck took him to Tony's, a famous restaurant in St. Louis. Everybody was respectful when Harry walked in and none of the customers bothered him while he ate. Of course, Harry was bothered about not being bothered because these were his people who were ignoring him. But when he stood up to leave, everybody in the place rose to applaud him. He was like Moses with his chosen people. He loved every moment of this.

After leaving the Cardinals, Harry would broadcast for the Oakland A's, but his high living expenses and his inability not to buy everyone in the house a drink with money from his expense account did not sit well with the penurious owner Charlie Finley. That gig lasted only one season. But then Harry came to Chicago and found a second home and base for power. He would broadcast for eleven years with the White Sox before making a smooth transition to the north side team in 1982. Dallas Green got him the job but told him, "Criticism is fine, but I won't stand for you to hop on my players for nothing."

As soon as Harry entered his booth at Wrigley, it was like he had been a Cubs fan all his life. Never had a broadcaster bonded so quickly with the home fans, who turned toward him in the seventh inning as he waved his microphone and led them in song. It was almost ritualistic. More than anyone, Harry Caray was responsible for the dramatic growth of the cult of the Cubs. "No one wanted the Cubs to win more than he did," said Cubs first baseman Mark Grace, the team's representative at Caray's funeral. "He didn't make any bones about it." Grace learned what being the team's most prominent cheerleader meant in terms of national recognition when he, Ryne Sandberg, and Andre Dawson—the team's three stars—signed autographs together inside the Astrodome in the late 1980s. "Harry peeked his head out of the dugout," recalls Grace, "and all of a sudden a hundred people moved away from us to get Harry's autograph. I knew then where he stood on the totem pole."

I listened to Harry often during his years with the Cubs. After his stroke in 1987, his speech pattern was impaired and I could tell he was different. But it didn't matter to me because there was still that familiar resonance and distinct sound that only Harry Caray could create. I could still enjoy him. What other broadcaster would blurt out, "How could a player from Mexico lose the ball in the sun?" Or, off the air, sit there with the biggest glass of vodka and explain, "The doctor told me I could have only one drink a day, but he didn't tell me anything about the size of the glass." Or tell wonderful stories, such as when he sent an ex-wife an alimony check with the note, "It seems like forever that I've been mailing you these checks. How long must this go on?" Her response was classic: "Dearest Harry—Until death do us part."

Well, Harry, the most human of all broadcasters, did part from us in 1998, before embarking on his fifty-fourth year in broadcasting. You talk about a guy who never left anything on the table—you can't live life any more fully than he did. The thought of baseball without Harry is inconceivable, so it made sense that the organist at his funeral had to learn a song he'd never played before. It was fitting that as Harry was carried away by the pallbearers, "Take Me Out to the Ball Game" resounded through the church. I'd like to think that they detoured on the way to the cemetery so they could swing by Wrigley Field.

Kerry Wood

Da bleacher bums were on their feet by the seventh inning at Wrigley Field on May 6, their tall cups of beer no longer perched on their bellies but raised toward the gray skies (despite the drizzle that mixed with the foam) in gleeful celebration of a phenom who was fulfilling impossible promise. Indeed, everyone in the sparse but extremely vocal crowd of 15,758, including those who scurried from their box seats to find shelter from the passing shower, was aware that they were witnessing baseball history being made by a baby-faced Cubs rookie pitcher who was still five months shy of being allowed to purchase his own brew. Kerry Wood, making only his fifth major league start, was in the process of throwing a one-hit 2–0 shutout against a very formidable Houston Astros lineup. But it was the flurry of strikeouts that kept the Wrigley faithful agog to the end. In fact, when Derek Bell waved helplessly at Wood's last pitch to close out the ninth, becoming the seventh straight batter to suffer this indignity, the twenty-year-old matched Roger Clemens's remarkable record of twenty strikeouts in a nine-inning game. Oddly, Wood was in such a zone during the glorious final three innings—"playing catch," as he'd later say, with receiver Scott Servais—that it wasn't until his postgame interview with Cubs announcer Steve Stone that he learned he had eclipsed his own personal high of fourteen strikeouts in a game, which he'd done as a kid back in Grand Prairie, Texas.

Wood, the Cubs' top pick and the overall number four pick in the June 1995 draft, had sent 329 batters in just 273⅓ innings of minor league ball back to the dugout shaking their heads. But despite all the hype that preceded him to the big leagues, he wasn't supposed to strike out twenty major league batters in a game, while giving up only a weak single and walking none! It is hard to argue with those who claimed that this was the most dominating pitching performance in baseball history. The young Texan, who was born just one town away from Ben Grieve, his Rookie-of-the-Year counterpart in the American League, was more modest about his masterpiece, saying sincerely, "I'm going to give most of the credit to the fans," because they were on their feet for every two-strike pitch. As Cubs first baseman Mark Grace would comment, "He doesn't know how good he is."

Wood's feat took everyone in Chicago by surprise, which explains the small crowd. If anything, Cubs fans have learned patience, and they assumed that all the predicted big strikeout performances and low-hit games promised by the Cubs' publicity department would begin happening a couple of years down the road. After all, they had seen Wood's four previous appearances, when he had an abysmal 5.89 ERA. Furthermore, some believed that the Chicago brass had been correct when it had explained to the press that Wood wasn't mature enough to begin the season on the major league roster. They didn't understand that a lot of organizations will send a rookie pitcher to the minors at the beginning of a season to make one start, before being recalled, because that will mean it will take him four years instead of three to qualify for arbitration. Having been wowed by Wood in the Cactus League, Anaheim manager Terry Collins scoffed at the reason the Cubs announced for sending Wood to Iowa to begin the season, joking that the Cubs were definitely going to be world champions since their management believed it had five starters who were better than Kerry Wood.

Wood's gem against the Astros was a rite of passage, of sorts. From that game on, he looked like he had been pitching in the majors for years, going 10-4 the rest of the way and showing near invincibility before the swelling home crowds. He lowered his ERA to a respectable 3.40, and held hitters to an NL-low .198 batting average. There were numerous highlights along the way. In fact, on May 11, he struck out thirteen Arizona Diamondbacks while earning a 4–2 victory, giving him thirty-three in two consecutive starts to break the major league record of thirty-two established by Luis Tiant in 1968 and later equaled by Nolan

Ryan in 1974, Dwight Gooden in 1984, and Randy Johnson in 1989. Late in May he'd strike out thirteen Braves in seven innings and two months later he'd shut them out in a 7⅔-inning stint, winning a highly anticipated duel with Greg Maddux. In his twenty-fifth start against the Reds on August 26, he recorded sixteen strikeouts in a 9–2 victory, and five days later, in his final start before being sidelined with an arm injury, he fanned ten Reds and belted his second homer of the season to help his own cause. Despite missing the final month of the season, Wood set the Cubs' seasonal rookie strikeout record with 233, and significantly became the first Cubs pitcher to strike out 200 batters since Fergie Jenkins set down 263 in 1971.

I would say that the Chicago Cubs have never had a pitcher like Kerry Wood. And to say that after only one season, instead of seven or eight, shows you what kind of phenom he is. I can say assuredly that no starting pitcher in the organization has been characterized by the strikeout since Jenkins. And though Jenkins, the last great Cubs starter, was also right-handed, he was a totally different pitcher. He struck out batters with guile and extraordinary control, rather than power. His little cut fastball to right-handed batters was devastating. The batters knew it was coming almost every pitch but they just couldn't handle it because they couldn't believe that he would be that consistent in hitting a little bitty zone that was only a little bigger than the ball. Fergie won twenty games in six straight seasons even though he didn't scare anyone. He'd give batters a comfortable 0-for-4. Wood, on the other hand, makes batters very uneasy. In order to intimidate, he will throw his 97-mph fastball inside. Usually only veteran pitchers understand how uncomfortable batters are when you force them to move their feet away from the plate.

I think it was appropriate that Wood equaled a record of Roger Clemens because that's the pitcher Wood most reminds me of, despite all the comparisons that have been made to that other Texan, Nolan Ryan. I always respect the opinions of Astros manager Larry Dierker, who, after Wood mowed down his team, contended that the phenom's fastball recalled the Ryan Express: "By the time the ball left his hands, it was in the mitt." And I know how it has been written that Wood's father, Gary, was a Ryan fanatic and that it was the strikeout king that he had his son emulate. And that Wood's Cubs jersey bears Ryan's number, 34. But it was the publicity-conscious Cubs who assigned Wood that number, and Wood himself has stated that as a youth he eventually looked more toward Clemens than Ryan as his model.

I can't help but think of the young Clemens when I watch Wood. He, too, has that confident demeanor and poise on the mound, a determination to throw inside, and a tremendous drive from the lower part of his body. He is even built like Roger, with those thick legs and big rear, so significant to lower-body power. From watching Clemens (and Ryan) as a kid, Wood knew the importance of building up his legs and allowed his dad to fit him with a special harness so he could drag tires around his school's football field. That shows you what kind of dedication he had. Fortunately, hard work has paid off for Wood in the same way it has for Clemens.

The sudden emergence of Wood into the baseball players' pantheon recalls when Dwight Gooden broke in with the New York Mets and toyed with batters. Doc had 276 strikeouts as a nineteen-year-old in 1984 and 268 strikeouts as a twenty-year-old in his 1985 Cy Young season, when he went a staggering 24-4 with a 1.53 ERA. Both pitchers displayed very effective fastballs that were up in the strike zone, from the waist to the letters. But Doc never had command on both sides of the plate. So when batters started laying off the high heater and he had to bring the ball down to try to get called strikes, he threw easier-to-hit fastballs over the middle of the plate. Wood is better at throwing unhittable low strikes; he may not have the control of Jenkins but when he has two strikes on a batter he can hit the outside part of the plate with his fastball. Gooden could overpower batters, but he couldn't freeze them with the called strike as often as Wood can. That was evident in the fifth inning of Wood's twenty-strikeout game when Moises Alou took three straight called strikes, Dave Clark then took three straight called strikes, and after fouling off two pitches, Ricky Gutierrez also was out on a called strike.

Their curveballs are much different. The young Gooden had a terrific curve to right-handers but his curve to left-handed batters would flop over the outside of the plate and be quite hittable. Wood has a wicked, wicked curve that causes batters on both sides of the plate to have fits. Wood doesn't throw the twelve-to-six off-the-table curve that a Darryl Kile or Tom Gordon possesses, but a sweeper. A batter can't catch up to it because it's exploding when it is in the strike zone. It is an example of a breaking ball that never stops. It continues to break in the glove, not just as it crosses the plate. That's what "action" is.

When you see Wood go back and forth between his hard curve and his blazing fastball (and he also has a nasty slider in his repertoire), you know why batters are at a decided disadvantage facing him. Which may explain why he seems so self-assured on the mound. As Jim Frye would say, "You give me a fastball and curve like that, and I'll be poised too."

While I acknowledge that Wood, along with Ben Grieve, was the young player last year who most heartened fans about the future of baseball, I don't want to anoint him a surefire Hall of Famer yet. It's strange to talk about Kerry Wood and greatness over a long period of time because he throws so hard at such a young age. You have to wonder if the arm is built to throw that hard this early in his career. A position player can adapt if he comes up with a sore arm, but if a pitcher's arm goes bad there is nothing he can do to compensate. He can no longer make a living. Hard throwers just hope pitching at full throttle doesn't take its toll on the arm. Wood might very well fall into the trap of trying for strikeouts every time he gets two strikes on a batter just to please the fans who urge him to do so. It's a temptation that could lead to arm trouble. On the other hand, I hope that the Cubs aren't planning on asking him to ease up in order to prolong his career. You may remember how the Mets asked Dwight Gooden to "economize on pitches" in his third season, telling him to deemphasize strikeouts and let his fielders record the outs. And I thought, "Uh, oh. Hitters won't always cooperate on that." What does *economize* mean? That you have batters bounce the ball to short? But those expected grounders can turn into line drives to the outfield, or over the fence. It's the same thing when management asks a home-run hitter (Mike Schmidt comes to mind) to cut down on his swing in order to cut down on his strikeouts. It's the wrong approach and almost always backfires.

If a pitcher like Wood is locked into throwing hard and has good control and batters can't hit him, then why should he change? Why should he give up his advantage over the guy with the stick in his hand? If it turns out he won't pitch long enough to reach the Hall of Fame, then at least he'll give all baseball fans a lot of thrills in a short period of time. And, fitting for a shooting star, he'll go out in a blaze of glory. If a flamethrower named Wood is destined to burn himself out, then so be it. So what should be done to protect one of baseball's hottest properties? Nothing.

Mike Piazza

If anybody would have asked me two years ago which superstar other than Cal Ripken, Jr., and Tony Gwynn was the most likely to play his entire career with the same organization, I might have said the Dodgers catcher Mike Piazza. Like Tommy Lasorda, a lifelong friend of Mike's father, Piazza seemed to bleed Dodger Blue. Having been drafted out of high school by the Dodgers (as a favor to Lasorda) as their 61st selection and the 1,390th overall pick in the 1988 draft, Piazza played several years in their minor league system before he joined the parent club and surprisingly became the Rookie of the Year and a perennial All-Star, put up Hall of Fame numbers, and emerged as the team's handsome and charismatic poster boy. Basking in popularity, making television appearances in everything from *Baywatch* to the soap *The Bold and the Beautiful,* Mike seemed content to stay put in L.A. Yes, he was asking for the largest contract in baseball history to remain in Los Angeles once his contract ran out at the end of the 1998 season, but it seemed unlikely that the Dodgers would let their franchise player get away at any cost. It was as impossible a scenario to imagine as the O'Malleys selling the team that had been in their family for more than four decades.

Yet the O'Malleys did shock the sports world by selling the Dodgers to media magnate Rupert Murdoch in mid-March, initiating a tumultuous season in which GM Fred Clare and manager Bill Russell would be handed their walking papers and Piazza would be sent packing. The sale of the team was the beginning of the end for Piazza as a Dodger because the new ownership hadn't the attachment to him that would have made his signing imperative. "It's unfortunate to see the way the Dodgers have lost the separation from the other organizations," Piazza would later comment. "The old regime set it apart. Now it's obviously a bottom-line business. They're only seeing the paper part of things, not the emotional part. To me, that's the disappointing thing." Oddly, what the Dodgers would give outsider Kevin Brown after the 1998 season would be about $25 million more than Piazza's asking price, yet they were willing to say so long to the player who had set almost every Dodgers single-season hitting record. But first they waited while his popularity with Dodgers fans diminished. It didn't take long because the press vilified him for wanting so much money to stay and for breaking off negotiations. Forget what he'd done in the past; now he was called a greedy "poison apple" without loyalty to team, teammates, or fans.

Many of the fans believed what they read and turned on their one-time hero. As their boos and catcalls rained down on him, the frazzled Piazza understandably struggled early in the year. But as he would do so often in '98, he overcame his personal travails and started hitting in the clutch, even belting three grand slams in April to tie the major league record. While giving himself the proper send-off, he also reminded the Dodger fans why they had appreciated his efforts since 1992. I think that by the time he was traded, the fans blamed the team more than Piazza for his departure. Ever the classy guy that he is, Piazza took out a full-page ad in the *Los Angeles Times* to thank them for their support over the years. Piazza paraphernalia would continue to sell briskly at Dodger Stadium even after he was gone; and when he returned in another uniform, he received a hero's welcome akin to John Glenn's when he returned from outer space.

Mike Piazza and his .331 lifetime average departed the Dodgers on May 15 in a blockbuster trade that involved the highest group of salaries ever in a transaction. He and third baseman Todd Zeile went to the Florida Marlins and Gary Sheffield, Bobby Bonilla, Jim Eisenreich, and catcher Charles Johnson came west. Surely the disorientation Piazza felt putting on a new cap and jersey was heightened because he knew that the Marlins, who were unloading all their high-salaried players, had no intention of keeping him. To his credit once again, he worked and played hard although he knew that he was headed elsewhere. It was probably somewhat of a relief that the fans in Florida weren't judging him on every at-bat, as had sometimes been the case in L.A. But of course, this might have been because the Marlin fans had been driven to complete apathy by the cruel fire sale of the players who had brought them a world championship in 1997.

A week after he arrived in Miami, on May 22, Piazza was informed he had been dealt again, this time for prospects. Now he was headed to the New York Mets, who had lost their star catcher Todd Hundley to off-season elbow surgery. It seemed like the ideal destination for a star accustomed to glamour and glitter. He was simply moving from Hollywood to Broadway. Mets fans, long deprived of a marquee player, were so excited that there was a standing ovation at Shea Stadium when Piazza's acquisition was announced, and when he made his debut for the Mets on May 23, Shea had its first sellout in five years. After his treatment in L.A., Piazza couldn't help but be exhilarated by the thunderous applause he received every time he strode to the plate. And he must have wondered if this was how it would be for as long as he was a Met. When the Mets immediately came alive and went on a hot streak, putting up crooked numbers in bunches, the large crowds could not have been friendlier to Piazza and patiently waited for him to break out in a big way.

However, when the Mets cooled off and returned to playing like they did before Piazza's arrival, the fans began to sour on the player who was supposed to be the savior. Every time he failed to produce with men on base, he was booed heavily, by more and more fans. Piazza was perhaps the first player ever to experience bicoastal booing from home crowds in the same season! You could see the joy that he felt when he first came to New York disappear from his face. And every time he did homer or drive in a key run, he refused to show any emotion, as if he were saying, "Yeah, you're cheering me now, but I heard those boos when I walked to the plate."

I saw Piazza on a regular basis and could tell that he was not having fun. I'm sure there came a time when he was just counting the days until the end of the season and thinking about signing with another team for 1999. The fans were driving him out of town. At least the fans in Los Angeles had booed him because of his salary demands, but that wasn't the case in New York. Piazza is a tough, hardworking individual who plays hurt and does all the things you want from your superstars, yet he was booed for no apparent reason at Shea other than, "Hey, you're not hitting right now." Maybe if he weren't replacing (and eventually displacing) the popular Hundley, the fans would have been more tolerant, but it was as unfair treatment as he could have received.

Perhaps he learned from team leaders Al Leiter, Lenny Harris, and John Franco how to deal with New York's most vitriolic fans, because Piazza was able to come out of his funk, look like he loved the game again, and be an amazing force during the last six weeks of the season. As he began to put on an incredible display of clutch power hitting, his new attitude was a refreshing "I might as well get booed by the best if I was going to get booed by anyone." It wasn't just the impressive numbers he put up, but the way he delivered for his new team with dramatic flair. Sometimes the only way the Mets could win was if he'd hit a home run. And he'd do it. If the team desperately needed an RBI late in the game, he'd give it to them. And everyone would say, "Well, can he do it again tomorrow?" And he'd do it again. "How many times can he do it?" Well, he'd do it again. It seemed like every other game that the Mets won, it was Piazza's bat that won it for them.

Equally impressive was how Piazza was handling himself behind the plate. He isn't the defensive catcher that a healthy Hundley is, but he did an admirable job and showed Hundley's toughness. He was beat up behind the plate on a daily basis but was remarkably resilient. As a matter of fact, in August he was struck so hard in the groin that his protective cup cracked. "I was catching sidesaddle for a couple of games," Mike said. It wasn't just the foul tips and the plays at the plate, but having to block balls in the dirt. In Los Angeles, he mostly caught pitchers who threw high fastballs, straight changes, and curveballs, none of which are pitches with bite. However, on the Mets, he caught pitchers who threw sliders, sinkers, and splitters in the dirt. The Dodger pitcher who most frequently threw the splitter was Hideo Nomo, and he joined the Mets later in the season. So Piazza got no relief. He was always going down in the dirt to prevent pitches from bouncing away and was repeatedly being hit by balls shooting off the hard ground. Still he hung in there.

I found it interesting to see how the Mets fans changed as it became clear that Piazza was as great as his reputation, and was arguably better than anyone on the cross-town rival Yankees. It became evident that the majority of fans in New York who boo a hometown player don't want him to fail, but to prove his mettle by overcoming their hostility. They want to challenge a player to turn their cheers into boos. However, this questionable "strategy" for stimulating players to perform at their peak almost backfired with Piazza. When he started playing even better than they had hoped, it dawned on them that the booing had gone on for so long that he wouldn't be flattered by their sudden appreciation of him. They worried that they had so angered him that he'd ignore the cheering and leave the team at the end of the year. It was amusing when fans in the stands would try to quiet anyone who was still booing because they feared Piazza would be further turned off to playing in the Big Apple. When Piazza began voicing excitement about his new team being involved in the wild-card race with the Cubs (and eventually the Giants), Mets fans, sensing he might be coaxed into returning in 1999, would call up radio talk shows and tell other fans to cease their negativity toward him. One fan, perhaps hoping Mike was listening in, would insist, "It's a minority of people who are booing." The next fan would counter with, "No, it's ten thousand people." But the third, pro-Piazza fan would counter, "Well, nobody was booing where I sat."

I know that through the debate, the Mets' ownership was delighted that the team was getting attention that ordinarily would have gone to the championship-bound Yankees. And I'm sure the fan reaction to Piazza was instrumental in the Mets' making an enormous contract offer to him after the season. I was among those who was surprised that Piazza accepted the seven-year deal and voiced enthusiasm about playing with the Mets for the rest of his career. I'm sure the fans, who I believe learned something about themselves last season, drew a collective sigh of relief that Piazza had indeed forgiven them.

Piazza showed the Mets fans what the Dodgers fans had almost forgotten: that he is a sensational hitter who doesn't just do well when things are in his favor but is most impressive when the odds are against him. That he overcame as many hardships as he did during the 1998 season and still batted .328 with 32 homers and 111 RBIs is the mark of a man. If there were such a prize as the Most Courageous Player of the Year Award, Mike Piazza would have received my vote for 1998.

David Wells

I always wondered how difficult it would be to explain
to a new baseball fan why a perfect game is so exciting.
After all, absolutely nothing happens. It would just get
more complicated if the fan suddenly became too clever
and asked questions like "Why do they call it a perfect
game if all twenty-seven batters don't strike out on three
pitches?" And, "How come the pitcher isn't perfect-
looking?" Fittingly, the perfect season, 1998, had its perfect game and, as fate would have it, the stands were
loaded with baseball neophytes who were there only for a
Beanie-baby giveaway, and the pitcher they saw throw the
gem, David "Boomer" Wells, had the bearing of someone in
a Saturday afternoon beer league.

It's true that some of the 49,820 people who bought

tickets to the Yankees-Twins game at Yankee Stadium on May 17 foolishly dropped their stubs in the gutter, corralled their kids, and zoomed off in their minivans after they got their hot collectibles. But I'm sure that those other nonfans who stuck around soon understood that what they were witnessing was out of the ordinary and downright thrilling. Because *everybody* in the large crowd was yelling themselves hoarse from early in the game, when Wells began to show a complete mastery over the Twins batters, and *everybody* was tense as the game neared its conclusion. No-hitters-in-progress are funny in that for no good reason nobody wants to jinx the pitcher by letting him know what he's doing (as if he didn't know). But the cheering was so thunderous—perhaps inspired by the interlopers who didn't know the "no-hitter rules"— that it was obvious this crowd had no intention of keeping Wells uninformed. They even gave him a standing ovation as he headed to the mound to begin the ninth inning. It was okay—Wells had already relaxed after his pal David Cone teased, "Don't walk anybody." In total control of his pitches and emotions, the left-hander wouldn't walk anybody on this day, going to three balls on only four batters. Only two pitches were hit hard all day, and none in an easy ninth inning.

In the ninth, Wells retired rookie Jon Shave on a routine fly to right fielder Paul O'Neill, recorded his eleventh strikeout against Javier Valentin, and got Pat Meares on another fly to O'Neill, and it was over. As the crowd rocked the stadium, Wells punched his left fist twice toward the ground, and as he was being carried off the field by his jubilant teammates, pumped his hat triumphantly toward the sky (in tribute to his late mother, Eugenia Ann). Wells had pitched only the thirteenth perfect game in major league history in beating Minnesota 4–0. Moreover, he became the only pitcher in Yankee history to toss a perfect game other than Don Larsen, who, after a night on the town, dominated the Dodgers at the Stadium in the 1956 World Series. Those who don't believe that the stars were in the "perfect" alignment should consider that Wells and Larsen both attended Point Loma High School in San Diego and that Joe Torre, as a young spectator and then as the Yankees' manager, attended both games.

With the rare perfect game, the beefy, tattooed, disheveled, free-spirited advocate of hot music and cool beer—the kind of guy you'd follow around with a coaster at a party—gained eternal respectability in baseball annals. Wells, who physically resembles his idol Babe Ruth (and once wore Ruth's cap, which he purchased for $35,000, for an inning), also became an instant human metaphor for a perfect season that was full of but not marred by imperfections.

Of course, a perfect game equals only one victory, but in Wells's case it resulted in many victories because it turned around his season. He had come into the game with a 5.23 ERA, but from that time forward he was virtually unbeatable, finishing the season at 18-4 with a 3.49 ERA and then thriving in the postseason. In fact, later in the season he almost threw a second perfect game against the Oakland A's before losing it in the seventh inning! He swore he had better stuff that day than when he did pitch his perfecto. That one game on May 17 told him that he could be a great pitcher. And for the rest of the season he pitched with a confidence that had been lacking throughout his entire career. He had complete faith in his four-seam fastball, excellent circle change, and curve; wasn't afraid to pitch inside; and had stupendous control, walking only 29 batters (while striking out 163) in 214⅓ innings.

Early in 1997, I was telling everyone during broadcasts that the Yankees made a big mistake letting free agent Jimmy Key go after they won the 1996 championship, and then trying to make up for that gaffe by signing Wells, whose record had never equaled his talent over ten seasons with Toronto, Detroit, Cincinnati, and Baltimore. I said that I thought the Yankees were just desperate to sign any left-hander after Key's departure. After Key won eight of his first nine starts with the Orioles, I was one of the people saying "I told you so." But George Steinbrenner's "people" told him Key would break down in a couple of years, and that is what happened. (In fact, Key announced his retirement in January 1999.) Like everybody else, I ate a lot of crow last year as I saw the emergence of a standout pitcher in New York. (Wells's stock rose so much that the Yankees were able to trade him—along with Homer Bush and Graeme Lloyd—before the 1999 season for the American League's best pitcher, Roger Clemens.)

Not only did Wells become the Yankees' ace by the end of the season, ahead of twenty-game winner David Cone and Andy Pettitte, but this rebellious outsider also assumed a position of leadership on a team that was on its way to the world title and 125 victories. As Tom Verducci of *Sports Illustrated* wryly commented, "Wells' leadership qualities until recently had been limited to buffet lines." Verducci reported that Wells showed his regard for his teammates, Joe Torre and his coaches, and even Yankee front-office personnel by presenting them with specially designed diamond-encrusted rings to commemorate the perfect game. That was a surefire way to silence their disapproval for his blaring of music in the clubhouse.

Perhaps Wells hasn't made the full transformation from renegade to responsible citizen, but at least he's made the effort to put the team in front of his own ego. It hasn't been easy for Wells to come around even this far. The most positive influences on Wells have been David Cone and Joe Torre. When Wells was with previous teams, every time he'd exhibit some undisciplined behavior, people would say, "That's just Boomer," and shrug it off. As Cone told me, Wells, who never knew his father growing up, likes to test people in authority and if they don't challenge what he is doing, he'll keep doing it. That kind of attitude doesn't fly with the Yankees, particularly with Cone and Torre. I know Torre has spoken to Wells on several occasions when his pitcher has lapsed into a nonprofessional mode. Like the time in Baltimore when Wells looked angrily at his fielders for not catching a long-hanging fly. Or when after being relieved—after a 9–0 lead shrank to 9–7 in a game at Texas—he slammed the ball in Torre's hand. You don't show up your boss in front of forty thousand fans. Torre spoke firmly to Wells and he appreciated it. After the Baltimore incident he apologized to his teammates. After Texas he apologized to Torre. Two starts later he tossed his perfect game.

Cone says, "That's just Boomer, my ass." He reminded me of the 1997 incident in Miami when Wells came up to bat in the second inning and was ejected for arguing balls and strikes with the National League umpire. Cone confided that he went into the clubhouse and had a toe-to-toe screaming session with Wells about how he had been irresponsible to the team. How did Wells take the stern lecture? That's when he and Cone became friends.

Cone says their friendship is based on their being kindred spirits: "We're both flaky." Unfortunately, the word "flaky" is usually used negatively in sports—only in regard to Bill "Spaceman" Lee and Mark Fidrych has it been used endearingly. But Cone had pride when he used the word to describe himself and Wells. I think flaky can be good. I define flaky as abandon. You have the discipline to not be disciplined. You have the freedom of spirit to let your athletic ability come through. I think Cone impressed upon Wells that it was possible for him as a Yankee to continue to be a free spirit and free thinker and still be an integral part of the team. He made Wells realize that it was possible to be flaky and professional at the same time. I think that Cone and Torre, together, have given new direction to Wells, who had been a rudderless, devil-may-care, R. P. McMurphy character.

The greatest opportunity Wells has to express his freedom of spirit is on the mound. This guy has such abandon in his delivery. You'll notice when he follows through that there's no tautness in his motion. It's free and easy. I remember how Chris Short, the fine Phillies left-hander in the sixties, would come to spring training and throw two or three pitches after being off all winter and be ready to begin the season. I think Wells is the same way. He is able to be a workhorse because it would be hard to imagine him getting a sore arm or torn rotator cuff with that easy style of his. It's almost as if the freedom with which he releases the ball is meant to represent the freedom with which he tries to live his life. It may not be the conventional approach for a major league pitcher, but it sure is refreshing.

Dan Quisenberry

In a baseball season filled with emotional moments, there was none greater than on May 30, when more than thirty thousand fans in Kansas City paid loving tribute to Dan Quisenberry, the day's guest of honor. The reason for the one-time star reliever's appearance at Kauffman Stadium on that Saturday afternoon was ostensibly his induction into the Royals' Hall of Fame, but it was really so he could say good-bye to the fans and they to him. Diagnosed with brain cancer, the same dreaded disease that had claimed his former Royals manager Dick Howser, Quisenberry had acknowledged that he wasn't expected to live much longer, despite plans to soon undergo surgery for the second time. As he waved to the crowd with one hand and placed the other in the supportive grip of his proud, smiling wife, Janie, tears flowed freely throughout the ballpark. "I loved playing in front of you folks, great fans, great city, great team," he said. "This is more than I deserve. God bless you all."

When Quisenberry died on September 30, after enduring nine months of pain, I recalled what a longtime Memphis friend once told me: "It's only a tragedy if you die before you're fifty. After that it's sad when you pass but you've been given a chance to experience life in full." Well, Quisenberry lived to be only forty-five, and his passing was one of the most tragic stories of baseball in 1998.

As great a pitcher as he was for the super Royals teams of the eighties—and he led the league in saves five times, including in 1983, when he set a major league record with forty-five—he was regarded by everyone as even a better person. It's easy to be loved when you're at the end of your life, but Quisenberry was truly adored by everyone he came into contact with during his career. They would say of Dale Murphy that he was the only player in baseball who could count all of his twenty-four teammates as *good* friends, but the same could be said of Quisenberry. No one was more popular. And after he retired, his bond with the city became stronger. He was involved in many civic works, including an annual charity golf tournament, and collecting food for the hungry and homeless in Kansas City. He also began to write poetry and gave readings at local libraries and bookstores.

Teammates like George Brett and Frank White have said that what they remember most about Quisenberry was his sense of humor, how he kept everyone loose by making light of everything. He was known as somewhat of a trick-ster and I think that trait carried into his pitching. How he enjoyed baffling batters with an underhanded delivery and watching them swing upward as his wicked sinkerball went down. The rare closer who eschewed strikeouts, he wanted to fool overeager batters so they'd top the ball and hit grounders to his sure-handed infielders. Grounders de-lighted Quisenberry. "I lull [batters] into a false sense of se-curity by letting them watch me pitch," said the man who threw nothing above 85 mph. "If overconfidence can cause the Roman Empire to fall, I ought to be able to get a ground ball." For most relievers the mound is a pressure-cooker, but Quisenberry saw it as his platform to perform his com-edy act, with the batters being his foils.

Along with his wit and indomitable sense of fun, Quisen-berry won people over with his humility, his genuine feel-ing that he was the same as the people who filled the stands. As did Ken Tucker in his extremely touching obit-uary in *Baseball Weekly,* I will conclude with the telling words of Brad Newland, a Kansas City golf professional who worked with Quisenberry on the Harvesters charity tournament:

"He was a famous athlete, but he never acted like he was better than anybody else. . . . I have an autographed baseball Dan signed for me. Someday I'll be proud to show it to my 2½-year-old son. I'll be proud to tell him I knew Dan Quisenberry and I'll be even prouder if my son grows up to be as fine a man."

Juan Gonzalez

His twenty-fifth homer of the season came on a 1-2 pitch in the first inning and traveled roughly 430 feet over the left-center-field fence and gave the Rangers a 1–0 lead over the visiting Mariners. His twenty-sixth, which was blasted over the center-field fence, came on a 2-1 offering with two runners on in the bottom of the seventh and gave the Rangers a safe four-run cushion, 8–4. The imposing six-foot-ten-inch left-hander on the mound knew he had been beaten. Hitting two home runs in one game against Randy Johnson would be a memory most players would treasure forever. What made it even more special for Juan Gonzalez is that the 4 RBIs he accumulated against him in the Rangers' last game before the All-Star break made him only the second player in major league history to have over 100 RBIs prior to the mid-summer classic. And, as Gonzalez later exclaimed, "the first Latin player!" Only Hank Greenberg's 103 RBIs in 1935 topped the star outfielder's 101 runs batted in.

After the game Texas manager Johnny Oates expressed his elation over Gonzalez's accomplishment, demonstrating his respect for his star player. "The number one objective [each game] is for the team to win," he said, "but every once in a while you have a special night. You don't forget the team victory, but this game has been played for a long time and not too many guys have gotten one hundred RBIs before the All-Star break. It's a very special night for our organization and an extra-special night for Juan Gonzalez."

Even the losing manager, Lou Piniella, was impressed: "It's hard to believe Juan has more than one hundred RBIs already. One hundred used to be the barometer for a very successful season."

It was written the next day how after eighty-seven games Gonzalez was "on pace" to break Lou Gehrig's 1931 AL mark of 184 RBIs in a single season and to equal the major league mark of 190 set by the Cubs' Hack Wilson back in 1930. I've always had trouble with the term "on pace," because a batter could drive in five runs in his first game and be "on pace" to have 810 RBIs for the season. Some of the paces players are expected to keep to are unrealistic. To equal the record and to stay "on pace," Gonzalez would not be able to have even a minor RBI drought during the second half of the season. And that was not going to happen. Even a five-RBI game against Kansas City and a seven-RBI onslaught against Detroit wouldn't be enough to overcome a few minor swales. He would finish the season with an American League–best 157 RBIs in 154 games, the most in the junior circuit since Junior Stephens and Ted Williams each drove in 159 runners for the Red Sox in 1949. He fell only one RBI short of tying Sammy Sosa for the major leagues' best mark. And in addition to driving in over one hundred runs for the sixth time, he had over forty homers for the fifth time, including his thirty-fifth against Cleveland on August 20 that made him Texas's all-time hits leader. Everyone had wondered what Gonzalez would do if he played in over 150 games for the first time since 1992, and he didn't disappoint anyone. He had a sensational season and was deserving of winning the MVP for the second time, a first for a Hispanic player.

To have had 432 RBIs in 421 games over the last three seasons is an amazing accomplishment, especially when one considers how often Gonzalez, who hasn't been well insulated in the lineup, was walked or pitched around with men in scoring position. It's obvious that he rarely misses a pitch in his zone when he has the opportunity to knock in some runs. While Gonzalez bears down on every at-bat, what has elevated him into the "Great RBI Man" category is that with a man on third with one out or on second with two outs, his eyes light up. It's as if someone had thrown cold water in his face to alert him to the possibilities. What makes him so dangerous is he takes more pride in driving in runs than in hitting homers.

He hits the ball so hard that often just making contact

will result in a homer. Playing in Texas Stadium, all he
needs is to hit a line drive to reach the stands, which is
why he is a legitimate candidate to threaten single-game
and seasonal home-run records. He's just so powerful. In
fact, he has much better power to right field than Mark
McGwire. Like most Hispanic players, he's a free swinger
who likes to take a pitch on or just off the outside corner
and go the other way with it. Only he does it with astonishing power. I'm sure his being one of the first Hispanic
players to use weights extensively has made a big difference.

I have a fond memory of one of Gonzalez's colossal
home runs. It happened in February of 1995 in Puerto
Rico, where I'd gone to watch the Caribbean World Series.
Gonzalez was part of a Puerto Rican "dream team" that
was playing against a team from the Dominican Republic,
whose pitcher was Jose Rijo. Some of Gonzalez's star
teammates were Roberto Alomar, Carlos Delgado, Carlos
Baerga, Rey Sanchez, Ruben Sierra, and Bernie Williams—
it was a big deal. The stadium was packed with about
twenty-five thousand fans and there were seven or eight
little bands playing, so the atmosphere was festive and
electric. At the time Gonzalez, a marvelous physical specimen who had deservedly earned his reputation as a
ladies' man, was dating salsa queen Olga Tañon. Everybody in Puerto Rico knew about the affair, so Olga thought
nothing of appearing at this game to cheer on her man.
Soon she and the many Gonzalez idolaters in the stands
were on their feet when he launched a pitch way into the
night, halfway to Mars. Puerto Rico's first baseman Car-

melo Martinez, whom I had befriended when he played ball in the States, turned to me and said, "Nobody stronger, nobody stronger." And all I could say as I watched Gonzalez circle the bases was "I couldn't agree with you more." I don't know if Carmelo heard me because the bands had started to play. What had happened was that as Gonzalez rounded third, he broke stride and pointed toward Olga Tañon. The band then broke into her theme song and the crowd went wild as Olga stood up and waved, doing the whole Evita thing. What an unforgettable scene.

It's not surprising that Gonzalez is such a hero in Puerto Rico. Even Orlando Cepeda didn't put up the power numbers he does. But playing in Texas, he hasn't received anywhere near the attention in America that he does on his native island. He hasn't achieved, as Mark McGwire has pointed out, "the notoriety he should have" after putting up big numbers year after year. But it looks like that is about to change. The other players know how good Gonzalez is. And so do the opposing managers. For instance, before last year's Yankees-Rangers play-off series, Joe Torre told me, "You can't make a mistake against this guy." In baseball, when someone refers to someone else as "this guy," it has a different connotation. "This guy" takes the place of the name of someone who is very respected. And when Torre used the term to describe Gonzalez, I sensed he was referring to someone who was almost "bigger than life." When the manager of a team full of stars is awed by the talent of somebody on another team, you know that player's something special. I wouldn't be surprised if across the field in the other dugout, Texas manager Johnny Oates was gazing at the player Torre was talking about. And perhaps remembering all that Gonzalez had done during his MVP season, Oates smiled confidently and said to himself, "This guy is too good to be true."

Jose Canseco

Jose Canseco was playing the part every ballplayer learns very early in his career. As Dick Groat informed me when I was a youngster on the Cardinals and did a little too much chirping in the clubhouse after getting a couple of hits in a game, you are expected to take the role of the unselfish ballplayer and tell the press that your personal accomplishments mean squat because they didn't contribute to a victory. So on July 26, there was Canseco looking glum and grousing to the press about the Blue Jays' 6–3 loss to the Red Sox, although he had just broken the record for home runs by a non–American-born player during the game, hitting his 380th to move ahead of Orlando Cepeda and Tony Perez. "The record's nice," conceded Canseco. "The fact is we lost."

If Canseco did allow some ego to slip through when he pointed out, "But there will be more records down the road, there will be other power hitters I will pass," it's understandable. For this home run had to be a big deal to Canseco. After all, it made the Cuban-born thirty-four-year-old the all-time Hispanic home-run leader. Also it was the attention-grabbing homer in a season when Canseco would unexpectedly hit a career-high forty-six long balls. Signed at an extremely modest salary by the Blue Jays at the urging of Roger Clemens, he would have a season that was reminiscent of those he had early in his career with Oakland, when he became baseball's highest-paid player.

What Canseco's resurgent season reminded me of was the line "He finally said hello when it was time to say goodbye." The point being that it came too late. There had been too many years between his exciting years with the A's and 1998, during which time all anyone saw was wasted potential. Tony La Russa once professed that Canseco was the greatest talent that he ever managed, and that includes certain Hall of Famers Rickey Henderson and Mark McGwire. His belief seemed justified when Canseco was the A's MVP in 1988 after becoming the first player to hit forty homers and steal forty bases in a season. But La Russa's patience ran out on Canseco as he became an undisciplined player who was more concerned with entertaining the fans than playing smart winning baseball. In subsequent years with the Rangers, Red Sox, and Art Howe–managed A's, Canseco did nothing to prove La Russa's later, more negative assessment wrong. There were too many times when he struck out trying to awe the fans with gargantuan home runs, when all they wanted was a key base hit. And there was too much evidence of lackadaisical play—it doesn't often happen that a ball conks an outfielder on the head and bounces over the fence for a home run. Also Canseco got the reputation for being injury-prone. It truly is a shame how injuries robbed him of an enormous amount of playing time during his prime years. There were hand injuries, groin injuries, back injuries, rib injuries, and even a career-threatening ligament tear in his right elbow that he got after volunteering to pitch a meaningless inning in a blowout for the Rangers in 1993. If Canseco had stayed healthy, it's likely he would have had ten or eleven 100-RBI seasons instead of just six and over 500 homers already, so one understands why Canseco insists injuries are the reason he has lost his chance for the Hall of Fame. However, even if he finishes with Cooperstown-caliber power numbers, I think that when the voters assess his career, the other problems I've mentioned will hold him back far more than injuries.

What I think people in baseball and fans have found troubling about Canseco is that he has skills superior to almost anybody in the game yet has never seemed interested enough in being the great player he could have been. For people with lesser talent, it is incomprehensible that somebody would not want to be playing the game to the best of his ability all the time and for as long as he possibly can. Canseco was so good at such an early age that it would have been possible for him to have maintained that level of excellence only if he had been extremely dedicated. But since then Canseco has never dedicated himself to his craft. He was a victim of the game being too easy for him. He shows us flashes of amazing talent, but not the discipline to play the game properly. I'm not surprised that Toronto was willing to let Canseco go elsewhere during the off-season. Because even after last year, Canseco has a lot of work to do—and I do mean work—in order to shake his reputation for being the most productive hitter that nobody really wants.

Larry Doby
and Don Sutton

It was only a day after the Yankee organization welcomed prodigal son Jim Bouton to an Oldtimers Game after
exiling their former star pitcher for thirty years because of
"indelicate" remarks he'd made about some Yankee stars in
his groundbreaking exposé *Ball Four*. On July 26, Cooperstown finally enshrined Larry Doby and Don Sutton, two
deserving players whose exclusion from baseball's celes-
tial home had gone far beyond reason. The black descen-
dant of slaves in South Carolina and the white son of an
Alabama sharecropper expressed extreme happiness to be
inducted along with Negro Leagues pitcher Bullet Joe
Rogan, influential ninety-four-year-old African-American
sportswriter Sam Lacy, Dodgers Spanish-language broadcaster Jaime Jarrin, and executive Lee MacPhail. But who

could have blamed them if they still felt bitterness for not having been selected exactly five years after they retired?

Doby was a power-hitting second baseman with the Newark Eagles in the Negro Leagues when Bill Veeck, the maverick owner of the Cleveland Indians, boldly signed him to a major league contract, much to the disappointment of the Brooklyn Dodgers scouts who were in hot pursuit. On July 5, 1947, only eleven weeks after Jackie Robinson broke baseball's color barrier with the Dodgers, Doby became the second black player in the majors and the first in the American League. Because Doby was second, he didn't receive the same attention as Robinson and never was given due credit for helping Robinson pave the way for the many black players who followed in the next decade. Doby also had to endure racial taunts from fans at the ballpark and the redneck players in the opposing dugouts, and he received similar threatening hate mail. He, too, suffered the humiliation of being denied entry to hotels, restaurants, and other public facilities in various cities. Like Robinson, he was silent when expedient, defiant when necessary.

Doby didn't change the way baseball was played, as did the dynamic Robinson, who terrorized pitchers by being more aggressive with the bat and on the bases than anyone they'd ever seen. Still, he was an impact player who was a dangerous left-handed hitter and fine right-handed throwing outfielder. In 1949, Doby, Robinson, and Dodgers Roy Campanella and Don Newcombe became the first African Americans to play in the All-Star Game; Doby was the first to play for the American League. He'd play in seven All-Star Games overall, have eight consecutive years with at least twenty homers, win two homer titles, drive in one hundred runs five times, and lead the American League in homers and RBIs in 1954 when the Indians won 111 games and the pennant. He knew a lot about hitting, as I would learn when I played briefly for Montreal in 1972 and he was Gene Mauch's batting instructor. I also liked Larry a lot, which is why I was very happy for his induction.

It took a public campaign on behalf of Doby, beginning when he was honored in Cleveland at the 1997 All-Star Game, to get him into the Hall of Fame. It's too bad that the voters on the Veterans' Committee almost had to be embarrassed into approving Doby's admittance. I think Doby had earned his place in Cooperstown simply because of his mammoth role in the desegregation of baseball. But if good statistics are also needed for entry, then Doby was still qualified. I think voters who underrated Doby's social contributions also argued that his stats were just below what was needed for the Hall of Fame. But they didn't take into account his four years in the Negro Leagues, when he batted .378. Except in the case of Monte Irvin, voters have not combined the *two* careers of players who spent time in both the Negro Leagues and the major leagues. In Doby's case, his Negro League stats should have been enough to lift him over the top as a Hall of Fame candidate. Again, I think he already had the credentials. It was about time baseball thanked Larry Doby in the only appropriate way.

Don Sutton was denied entry to Cooperstown for four painful years before being voted in by a comfortable margin in his final year of eligibility. Just when the former pitcher thought he wasn't going to be voted in and was directing all his thoughts toward the survival of a baby daughter who was born sixteen weeks prematurely, he got word that he was finally considered good enough. "I had tears and goose bumps when I found out," said Sutton, "but I didn't have the anticipation for it [happening]."

Tell me how the writers could ignore Sutton's 324 career victories for four years. Since Walter Johnson and Grover Cleveland Alexander finished their careers in the late twenties, the only other right-hander to have won that many games was Nolan Ryan, and he pitched three more years than Sutton. That should have told them a great deal about his accomplishment—324 of anything is hard. Sutton qualified for the Hall of Fame on durability, consistency, and longevity alone. In twenty-three years, he never missed his turn in the pitching rotation for the Dodgers, Astros, Brewers, Athletics, Angels, and Dodgers again. There were complaints that Sutton won twenty games only once in a twenty-three-year-career (in 1976), but he was twice a nineteen-game winner, won in double figures twenty-one times, and had at least fifteen wins twelve times. That's how a pitcher wins 324 games.

His numbers are impressive. He struck out 209 batters in 1966, which was the most by a National League rookie since Alexander in 1911. His career total of 3,574 strikeouts ranks fifth in baseball history. In addition, Sutton ranks third with 756 starts, seventh with 5,281.1 innings pitched, tenth with 58 shutouts, and is tied with Ryan for twelfth in victories. Having pitched sixteen years for the Dodgers, he holds virtually every pitching record for a franchise that has been rich with pitchers. He was also a clutch performer in four league championship series and four World Series, though his most important victory might have been the last game of the 1982 season, a virtual play-off between Milwaukee and Baltimore, when he outpitched Jim Palmer to give the Brewers the AL East title. Perhaps Sutton gave the voters an excuse to exclude him from the Hall for so long because of self-deprecating remarks he made during his career. His most famous line was "Comparing me to Sandy Koufax is like comparing [famed L.A. car painter] Earl Scheib to Michelangelo."

It was said that the baseball writers were reluctant to give Sutton his due because he was so blatant about doctoring the ball yet threatened to go to the Supreme Court if he was disciplined by umpires. Ray Miller once said, "Sutton will [someday] throw a ball to the plate with bolts attached to it." Sure Sutton did things to the ball, but the writers should know that most pitchers do, and that many of them have been voted into the Hall of Fame. What most baseball people don't seem to understand is that it isn't enough to cut or sandpaper a ball. A pitcher still has to know how to control the pitch and make it move the way he wants. Sutton was one of the best at it. Keith Hernandez agrees with me that Sutton was one of the toughest right-handers we ever faced because he cut the ball and then had the uncanny ability to throw a high strike on an even plane. It wouldn't dip at all! So it was hard to get on top of and the batter would foul it back or pop it up. I admired his ability to throw that pitch.

But I don't want to give the impression that Sutton, who now broadcasts cable games for the Atlanta Braves, won so many games only because he scuffed the ball. He had exceptional control and an array of pitches that he threw on any count. He threw several fastballs, some really good curveballs, and a screwball that would move away from left-handed batters, and then he started throwing sliders and almost everything else in the book. In the Dodgers organization, he learned how to pitch. Then he proved that he had intelligence, poise, drive, and talent to win at the big-league level—324 times! That's like hitting over five hundred homers, maybe even six hundred homers. There's a good chance that victory total may never be equaled again.

Dennis Martinez

Every veteran player eventually realizes that his talents are eroding faster as the number of candles increases on his birthday cake. But in many cases he still hangs on, waiting perhaps for just one more day to shine as he did in his prime. Fortunately, the baseball gods were on the ball in the remarkable 1998 season, letting several players enjoy last hurrahs. One player was forty-three-year-old Dennis Martinez, who on August 9 won the 244th game of his career to break Juan Marichal's record for Latin American pitchers.

The twenty-one-year veteran got his big triumph while pitching for Atlanta against the Giants, Marichal's team, and in Marichal's home ballpark, Candlestick Park (now 3Com Park). Martinez put himself in line for victory by pitching a perfect eighth inning and keeping the score at 5–5. Then in the top of the ninth Chipper Jones's two-out two-run single off Jose Mesa made the final score 7–5 and chalked up the needed victory for the delighted Martinez. His was no small feat, particularly in Latin America, where the number 243 has had similar significance as 61 and 755 do here. And in Martinez's native Nicaragua, they danced in the streets to honor the first player from that country to play in the major leagues. Ever since his career began with the Baltimore Orioles, for whom he pitched from 1976 to 1986, Martinez has been a genuine hero there. Consider a scene in the compelling 1983 political thriller *Under Fire,* which was coscripted by former minor leaguer Ron Shelton (writer-director of *Bull Durham* and *Cobb*). In it a young Sandinista rebel in a Baltimore Orioles cap makes a deadly accurate left-handed toss of a grenade that wipes out a group of snipers, mercenaries who have come to Nicaragua in 1979 to fight for Somoza. When, a few minutes later, American photographer Nick Nolte compliments him on his left arm, his surprising reply is: "Koufax was good, but Dennis Martinez—he's the best. He's from Nicaragua."

"Martinez is an inspiration to our country," stated the Giants' Nicaraguan outfielder Marvin Benard after the game. "When they call him El Presidente, it's not for nothing. If he ran for *presidente* of Nicaragua, he'd probably win." No wonder the current president was quick to congratulate the soon-to-retire Martinez after the game.

Martinez's milestone victory didn't come without a huge struggle. He had passed Luis Tiant's 229 victories in

1995 to move into second place among Hispanic pitchers, only fourteen behind Marichal, but in his last few years with the Indians, Mariners, and Braves, victories were at a premium. He no longer had the great stuff that had been in evidence with Baltimore and, after beating alcoholism, with Montreal from 1987 to 1993, when he became an All-Star pitcher (and tossed a perfect game against the Dodgers in 1991). Yet he remained a major-league-caliber pitcher because he'd shrewdly mix his breaking balls and change-ups and do anything he had to in order to get batters out. Anything. It appeared to me that there was a sense of urgency in his delivery, as if he were thinking, "This might be the last time I ever pitch; this may be the last out I ever record." I believe he'd think that way hitter by hitter, even pitch by pitch. You could see the desperation in his eyes. But you could also see a competitive desire, an inner fire that sustained him. His hope was that he could do well just enough times to pass Marichal's mark.

Martinez finally tied Marichal's victory total on June 2, when he scattered twelve hits to defeat the Milwaukee Brewers 9–0, his thirtieth career shutout and first complete game since May of 1996. There was a whole lot of season left to break the deadlock, but he was shifted from starter to reliever and it took him two months and seven days to do it. But he did it.

What impresses me the most is that Martinez has pitched long enough and well enough to win more games than Juan Marichal. A great, great pitcher. Marichal was the toughest right-handed pitcher I ever faced. Pete Rose agreed. And we're not alone. So I don't care if Martinez won his 244 (now 245) games by hook or by crook or just by refusing to go away. Obviously, Martinez, who retired in February 1999, was never in the class of Marichal. He admits this himself and was angered by quotes attributed to him (and sent along to Marichal) about how his winning more games than the Dominican star proved he had a better career. He knows he has as much chance of joining Marichal in the Hall of Fame as a teenage boy has of hearing his mother tell him he doesn't need a haircut. So I'm glad he at least got something special at the end of his career. He deserved it.

Albert Belle

As was his custom after a game, he did not talk to the press. Big Bad Albert Belle instead played video games while his teammates gave out the quotes that were needed for the early editions. He saw no need to be friendly to the Chicago media simply because his RBI double in the fourth inning in today's 5–3 comeback victory over the A's put him in an elite group with Babe Ruth, Lou Gehrig, and Jimmie Foxx as the only men to hit thirty homers and drive in one hundred runs in seven consecutive seasons. So none of the beat reporters could find out if he was proud of the record or if the reason he had been on a torrid pace since early July was his anger over being snubbed for the All-Star Game. (Go figure—he was mad at being left off the team in '98, but when he was selected for the '97 game in Cleveland, he asked manager Joe Torre not to play him.) In fact, in that month, he slugged a Chicago White Sox single-month record sixteen homers, drove in thirty-two runs, and batted a Ted Williams–like .406.

Belle would remain red hot in the hottest months and in September. In fact, in the final game of the season he homered, singled twice, and drove in three runs in a home victory over Kansas City to complete his ravenous assault on the Chicago White Sox record book. In his second year with the team, he established new franchise marks with 49 homers, breaking teammate Frank Thomas's old mark of 41; 48 doubles; 99 extra-base hits; 401 total bases; and 152 RBIs, 15 more than Zeke Bonura, a more lovable Louisianan, had in 1937. He joined Sammy Sosa and Juan Gonzalez as the first major leaguers to surpass 150 RBIs since Tommy Davis had 153 in 1962. Although a relatively slow start prevented Belle from challenging for any major hitting titles, he led the American League in the second half of the season in all three Triple Crown categories with a .387 average, 31 homers, and 86 RBIs. Check those numbers again. I think that his eye-popping stats after the All-Star break—and I didn't mention that his slugging percentage was a Ruthian .816—were his way of serving notice on McGwire, Sosa, Gonzalez, Griffey, et al., that if they will be going after any records or titles in 1999 he'll be right there with them.

Ferocious and intense from the moment he steps to the plate, Belle would be a tremendous hitter under any circumstances, but he (and Frank Thomas) benefit more than anyone from the unwillingness of pitchers in the

American League to pitch sluggers inside. It's revealing that Belle led the league in the second half in almost everything but being hit by pitches and is not even among the leaders in that category. Orioles manager Ray Miller once pointed out to me how intimidated pitchers, especially young pitchers, are by this glaring behemoth with the imposing bat. (It's not surprising that the Orioles would sign Belle to a huge contract after the '98 season.)

Belle supposedly keeps a book on all pitchers, but why bother? He knows that everyone pitches him away and with those long arms and no fear of being brushed back he can easily reach balls on the corners and just off them. That has become part of his zone. Pitchers know they are at a disadvantage because he and not they owns the outside part of the plate, so they try to get ahead in the count with a quick strike. But Belle's smart enough to be ready for this—there is no better first-pitch hitter in baseball. More than anybody, Belle must be pitched inside, so the pitcher can claim the outside corner. Yet it's hard to get a pitcher to do this when he has recent memories of yielding a long homer into the left-field stands to Belle on an *outside* pitch. Of course, when I say inside, I mean so far off the plate that he can't pull the ball fair. In truth, Belle, like all power hitters, would prefer to extend his arms.

Perhaps Belle's greatest accomplishment in 1998 was to hit so well despite being the target of hecklers in every ballpark in the American League. A McCoy who has come uninvited to a convention of Hatfields would be treated far better. Even in ballparks known for civility, pure venom is spewed out at baseball's most unpopular player. Horrific things. And it's not uncommon for objects and garbage to be thrown at him when he is out in left field. We all remember Belle being barraged by all kinds of debris at Jacobs Field in 1997, when he returned to Cleveland for the first time since abandoning the Indians for bigger money with Chicago.

Even fans who know little about opposing players know about his numerous off-field troubles. And they know about his troubles with fans and reporters, particularly his much-publicized profanity-laced tirade against NBC sportscaster Hannah Storm before a World Series game in 1995. I still remember introducing myself to Belle about five years ago and having him look at me as if I were subhuman. I didn't really care, but I thought it was a shame that a guy who has so much talent should appear so joyless and so bitter.

I was skeptical when the Yankees courted Belle after the 1998 season when it looked like they were going to lose Bernie Williams. I think it was for show. I can't imagine they were really serious about signing him. For one thing, in Yankee Stadium, you really need a center fielder to patrol left field because it is so spacious, and Belle is an immobile outfielder who even has trouble catching balls hit right at him. And of course, the Yankees under Joe Torre have thrived because of team chemistry, so why would they want to bring in the biggest downer around? Yes, we've all heard some of his teammates say how they've grown to understand and love Belle—but talk to the player whose stereo system he trashed for playing music he didn't like. I think Belle's presence could absolutely destroy a ballclub.

I assume that Belle will always be in demand as long as he puts up phenomenal numbers. But I wonder what will happen when he begins to slip. Nobody, particularly a maligned reporter, is going to give him the benefit of the doubt, and nobody will make excuses for him, as they would with someone they've long admired. You're not going to see any favorable articles written or hear kind words about him. It will always be, "He was a tremendous hitter, but . . ."

Joe Torre

To the casual observer New York's 7–0 victory over visiting Minnesota on August 11 was notable strictly because David Wells, who upped his record to 15-2, had thrown his perfect game against these same Twins at Yankee Stadium on May 17. Otherwise, it appeared to be just one more victory chalked up by a team that was in relentless pursuit of the American League record. However, to the Yankee players and manager Joe Torre it was a special occasion. In winning their 86th game of the season against only 29 defeats, the Yankees gave Torre a present to cherish: a .500 lifetime percentage as a manager. In his seventeenth year, his record stood at 1,168 wins and 1,168 losses. Torre had to be delighted because for the fourteen years prior to his becoming the Yankees' manager, his record was a seemingly unrectifiable 894-1,003, 109 games under .500. But after only five winning seasons in all those years—none with the Mets (from 1977 to 1981), two with the Braves (from 1982 to 1984), and three with the Cardinals (from 1990 to 1995)—Torre was in the midst of having his third consecutive high-victory season with the Yankees. Having taken only the 1982 Braves to the play-offs, he was leading the Yankees into the postseason for the third straight year and to their second world championship in three years.

When Warren Spahn was inducted into the Hall of Fame in 1973, Casey Stengel was present to honor baseball's winningest left-hander because he had managed him early in his career with the Boston Braves and late in his career with the New York Mets. Both teams were dreadful (as was the first team Stengel managed, the Brooklyn Dodgers), a far cry from the great Yankee teams Stengel managed to ten pennants and seven world titles from 1949 to 1960. Always ready with a quip, Spahn sent Stengel into convulsions of laughter by saying during his speech, "Casey managed me before and after he was a genius." Of course Spahn was joking, but the implication was that since Casey won only when he skippered the Yankees, he could win only if he had the horses. I was reminded of this in regard to Joe Torre, because it might be easy for future baseball historians to look at his overall record and assume that the only reason he became a successful manager with the Yankees was that he finally had a great group of players.

That assumption would be wrong. Torre has had super players since he joined the Yankees, but he richly deserved being selected Manager of the Year in both 1996 and 1998. In the voters' eyes, the Yankees' high number of wins in both seasons called attention to Torre's contribution rather than camouflaging it. I don't think that in his early days as a manager he should have been called "Clueless Joe," as the press often did, but he wasn't a great manager with his previous three teams. In fact, if he had remained just a fair manager, the Yankees wouldn't have fared nearly so well from 1996 to 1998 (and that's assuming that George Steinbrenner wouldn't have fired him after a poor showing in '96). It is only since he has been the Yankees' manager that Joe has blossomed from a manager with great potential into a great manager.

I've never told Joe this, but the manager he has been with the Yankees is the one I expected him to become long before. I knew how he thought and how he operated. My one-time Cardinals roommate was too unassuming to have the same expectations, because often you don't see yourself as others do. In any case, he took a long time to figure out how good he could be. Now he knows.

There is a period of adjustment for any ex-player who becomes a manager. I don't think Torre really understood what it took to be a good manager when he was with the Mets because those teams rarely rewarded smart managing with victories. But Torre did start to develop in Atlanta, though he never had the full support from Braves owner Ted Turner. I think when the volatile Turner fired him, Torre was devastated because, if anything, he merited a new multiyear contract for how much he and his team had improved. However, it may have been a blessing in disguise because during Torre's subsequent five-year stint as a broadcaster for the Angels, he was able to study and analyze the game from a distance, as well as learn about modern-day players and managers and how to deal with the media.

When Joe was ready to rejoin the managerial ranks, he accepted the job in St. Louis, where he had many of his best years as a player—including his remarkable 1971 season, after which he was voted the NL's MVP for leading the league with 230 hits, 137 RBIs, and a .363 average. Unfortunately, it wasn't in St. Louis that Torre revealed that he had become a better manager, because in his years under the parsimonious, autocratic rule of the Cardinals, Joe understood that he had neither the money nor the power to run the show. Surprisingly, Joe thrived instead in New York while working for George Steinbrenner, the owner famous for his revolving door of managers. He came back to New York, near where he grew up in Brooklyn, as a manager who had guile, guts, and a philosophy on how a manager should manage and players should play the game. He was a bottle of wine, perfectly aged—it was time to pop the cork. New York is the toughest town to conquer, but it comes with a stage that is ready for extraordinary performances—and that's what Joe gave from day one. He was book smart and street smart and had media savvy. The press, for whom he always had time and to whom he spoke with graciousness and wit, wrote only glowing articles about him. To paraphrase Harvey Araton of *The New York Times,* within two years he would become in many respects the paternal face of New York sports. The appreciative fans made him the city's unlikeliest hero. At a time when self-promotion is continually forced down our throats and it is difficult to separate a man from the spin, Torre proved a self-assured, comfortable fit. We were not fascinated with his hair, not bullied by his bluster. We just liked the idea of a man with a Brooklyn Little League named for him. Not only was he a manager of rich professionals, but also a model for those who coach our kids.

And what about his players? Did they respond positively to his soothing supervisory presence? Well, Torre brought such peace and tranquillity into the Yankee clubhouse that it's hard to believe that what had been the setting known as the Bronx Zoo became a school for higher learning.

Under George Steinbrenner, managers had always been hired just to be fired, and nobody predicted that Torre would last three seasons. He hadn't even been Steinbrenner's first choice for the job, so at best he was on probation. The reason Torre could work under such circumstances is that he hadn't expected to get the top manager's job in the big leagues, so he felt that there was nothing to lose. His main priorities at the time were his wife, Ali, who has been an enormous help to him; their baby, Andrea Rae; his older brother, Frank, who needed a heart transplant; and his other brother, Rocco, who died during the emotional '96 season. Against that background, Joe just went to work each day without feeling intimidated by Steinbrenner and worrying if George's much-used ax was about to fall again. He had nothing more than a respectful fear of George.

With the victories came confidence, but that has never meant Joe could be at ease while managing. Older brother Frank, who received his transplant during the 1996 postseason, made this comment about his younger brother near the end of '98: "You know a lot of people are saying this has been a cakewalk season, but I wish they could feel what my brother feels in his stomach when he goes to bed." I'm surprised Joe never gets an ulcer because when he sits in the dugout and seems stoical even during a game's tensest moments, his stomach is churning. In the heat of battle, players pick up on his wit and his calm, but underneath their manager is agonizing. When we were players he used to tell me that he wished he could be as fiery as I was because he would have loved to have exploded in anger in order to release all that tension that accumulated. The same holds true now that he is a manager. One way he tries to relax himself and keep his mouth moist is by sucking on a cherry pit. Another calming influence is his bench coach, Don Zimmer, who sits beside him every game. Popeye, who fires off ten or fifteen things at once into Torre's ear and maintains a cheery demeanor, represents—perhaps—the animation of Torre's personality.

Back when we were with the Cardinals, Joe and I whimsically discussed being co-managers some day, but we decided it wouldn't work because one guy and one guy only has to be responsible for all final decisions. But Torre and ex-manager Zimmer have been a perfect tandem. Zimmer is content just to give advice. And believe me, he gives a lot. After more than fifty years in baseball, Zimmer has an amazing feel for the game. He knows what other managers and coaches may and may not do in certain situations. Zimmer is so valuable because he is absolutely honest every time he answers Joe's questions, whether it's about strategy or a player's availability for a game. One of Torre's strengths is that he can respect what Zimmer has to say but take the responsibility of separating the wheat from the chaff.

Of course, Joe has numerous other strengths that make him such a successful manager. One major aspect of his style is to develop strategy based on the strengths of his players rather than the weaknesses of the opponents. That means he will have no problem with David Wells going with his high fastball against a high-fastball hitter like Paul Molitor at a key moment (rather than trying to throw something else in deference to him). Players appreciate such confidence from a manager.

The Yankees' style of play is a reflection of Torre, who had spent his entire career playing and managing in the National League. He was shrewd enough to encourage the Yankees to employ the aggressive through-the-bases running style of the senior circuit and then to turn them loose on unprepared American League opponents. After three years, this style still creates havoc. The Yankees don't have a lot of great base stealers, but everybody has the green light to steal and take the extra base. It's an exciting brand of baseball, in which the players feel they have the freedom to be creative.

Another way in which Joe has stamped his personality on these Yankees is by insisting that everyone plays for the team and not for themselves. He has been so convincing that players from all backgrounds have bought into this winning philosophy. They trust him enough to leave their egos at the door when they arrive at the ballpark, and this certainly has contributed to the team's chemistry. Even when a veteran player sits while a youngster takes his position, there are no complaints—last year it helped that Torre had the Midas touch when it came to knowing when to play youngsters like Shane Spencer, Ricky Ledee, and Homer Bush and when to stick with veterans like Chad Curtis, Tim Raines, and Darryl Strawberry. In the 1996 World Series, remember, he sat Tino Martinez, who had a great season, and went with Cecil Fielder at first base, a move that paid off. He was able to play Fielder without bruising Martinez's ego.

More than other managers, he works tirelessly to gain the confidence of his players. You see the Yankees' high victory total, but as in any big-league clubhouse, there are a lot of fragile players who need hands-on treatment. Torre is a firm believer that the manager's job is to work on the mental aspects of the game more than the mechanical. So when, for instance, Martinez was working too hard to get out of a slump, Torre tried to get him to ease up and not leave everything in the rehearsal hall. Simply put, the way he gets players to do this is by telling them he has enough confidence in their getting their grooves back that he will stick with them until they do. Last year, Martinez, Andy Pettitte, and a number of Yankees rewarded Torre for his loyalty with big performances at key moments. I like the way Torre deflects attention from young players like

Spencer and defuses controversy when it can damage a veteran like Chuck Knoblauch. Remember, Knoblauch was attacked by the press and by fans on the talk shows for allowing the winning run to score in a postseason game while he argued an umpire's call. He wants his players pressure-free so they can stay focused on their play.

I also like the way Torre will take the time to correct mistakes by players, firmly but without embarrassing them in front of teammates. When during a 1997 Fox broadcast, Jorge Posada hit a weak grounder and didn't bother to touch first base, our camera and microphone picked up Torre taking his young catcher aside to tell him in a quiet way about why he had made an out and then to tell him not to miss first ever again. It was typical Joe—a little coddling and then a strong point. It's little wonder that even the youngsters on this team quickly learn sound fundamental baseball.

Torre has made so few wrong tactical decisions with the Yankees that it seems like he has been waving a magic wand. The best example of brilliant yet subtle strategy by Torre last year took place in the fourth game of the 1998 World Series. It came in the eighth inning, when the Padres, who were trailing 5–2, had two men on base and the count went to 2-0 to the dangerous Ken Caminiti. That's when Torre lifted setup man Jeff Nelson and brought in closer Mariano Rivera. His reasoning was that since any Yankee pitcher would have to throw a fastball in this situation, why not go with the reliever who threw the best fastball? Rivera. It was sound reasoning. And I say that even though Caminiti singled to right off Rivera. He might have popped an expected Nelson fastball out of the park.

Incidentally, because Torre employed that type of strategy and masterfully used his pitchers and made lineup adjustments during the final six weeks of the season, the Yankees continued to win at an incredible pace. Joe Torre's Yankees finished the year with an AL-record 114 wins and only 48 losses. That meant Joe's lifetime record as a manager stood at a more respectable 1,206-1,187. And Joe, with a new contract in hand, would be back with the Yankees for his fourth year in 1999 to further improve on that. Let's see: 115 victories would up his total to . . .

Eric Davis

In baseball, and perhaps the everyday world as well, when a person becomes sick all the criticism of him comes to a screeching halt. Suddenly those traits of his that, on or off the field, disturbed everybody but the guy's mother are conveniently forgotten and those who know him best have upgraded the individual in question from being "a pretty good guy" to "a good guy" or even "a terrific guy." And when they look into a camera and address the player in his hospital bed with a reassuring "You're in our prayers," you can file those words in a folder labeled *BS*. I guarantee you that not one prayer will be uttered, at least not by them. Unless, perhaps, that afflicted player is Eric Davis. For him there were sincere sentiments and even prayers. That's because everyone who has met him (including myself) really does consider him a terrific guy.

I'm sure you know the story. Davis, signed to a free-agent contract by the Orioles before the '97 season, got off to a great start but had to leave his new team in May after being diagnosed with colon cancer. A third of his colon was removed during surgery in mid-June. It seemed so unfair, especially since Davis had lost so much of his career to injuries. Now those injuries seemed trivial. To everyone's surprise, Davis returned to the lineup in mid-September and for postseason play, despite having his strength sapped by chemotherapy. He not only played; he produced. It wasn't only about survival; it was about triumph. As he did numerous interviews during the postseason, one couldn't help but feel awed by his courage and touched by his humility. Davis was an inspiration, not only to the fans, but to his teammates and everyone else who played baseball. And to other victims of cancer and their loved ones. He would become an unofficial spokesman about the disease.

After Davis's dramatic appearance in the '97 postseason, I think a lot of us thought that might have been his swan song. No one would have been surprised if he took a full year off to put all his efforts into defeating the cancer and getting his strength back. When the Orioles picked up his option for 1998, many people assumed it was just a goodwill gesture. No one expected that Davis would come back in full force and become one of the greatest stories in a year of many great stories. Amazingly, the thirty-six-year-old right-handed batter hit a career-high .327, and after the

All-Star Game, when you would figure he would be showing signs of fatigue, he batted a robust .358! His greatest
moment came on August 15, when he went four-for-four in
a ten-inning victory over Cleveland and established an Orioles record by getting a hit in his thirtieth straight game.
That was the longest hitting streak in the majors last year.
Imagine!

Perhaps it is his power numbers, 28 homers and 89
RBIs in only 131 games, that are most startling. Those
were the type of stats Davis regularly put up as a budding
superstar with the Cincinnati Reds from 1986 to 1990.
When he first came up, I was among the many who said,
"Man, some talent," but I thought he held his hands too
low to ever be able to get around on pitches thrown above
his fists. Pitchers always gave him trouble with that pitch
and he struck out at an alarming rate, but he had such
quick wrists and bat speed that he became one of baseball's most dangerous hitters anyway. In 1987, the year he
really emerged, he smashed a career-high 37 homers, including an NL-record three grand slams in a month (the
record Mike Piazza tied in 1998). And he also displayed
brilliant speed and base-running talents, stealing 80 bases
(the next year he'd swipe 33 straight) to join Rickey Henderson as the only major leaguers to have 20 homers and
80 steals in the same season. Eventually he'd establish
himself as the greatest base stealer percentage-wise for
anyone in history with over 300 steals. In center field, he
displayed Gold Glove credentials.

It seemed that only injuries could prevent him from
making a serious run at Cooperstown. Unfortunately, in-

juries, particularly to his knees, struck him down with frightening regularity and kept him from ever playing more than 135 games in a season. Worst of all was a severe kidney laceration that he got from making a spectacular diving catch in the final game of the Reds' four-game sweep of the A's in the 1990 World Series. While his teammates went off to party and eventually go home for the winter, Davis was fighting acute pain for eleven days in an Oakland hospital, where he'd been abandoned by Reds owner Marge Schott. It's questionable whether he fully recovered because the next year he played in only eighty-nine games for the Reds and was a shell of the player he had been. He moved on to the Dodgers and Tigers but instead of regaining his old form, he came down with new injuries to his knee, wrist, shoulder, and neck.

After the '94 season he took a year off. It proved to be a wise decision. Healed, he returned to the Reds in 1996 and much to everyone's delight had an excellent season and captured his first Comeback Player of the Year award, prompting the Orioles to sign him to a free-agent contract. Not many players win this award more than once! That Davis conquered so much even before he got word of cancer makes you realize just how remarkable his comeback has been.

It was a shock when Darryl Strawberry was diagnosed with colon cancer in early October as his Yankees entered the play-offs. What were the odds that such good friends, sports teammates at Crenshaw High in L.A., would both be struck with the same life-threatening disease, at almost the same time? It was Davis's experience that prompted

Strawberry to have himself checked out at the first signs of pain, and this early detection, leading to early surgery, is the reason Strawberry's prognosis is so positive. As terrifying as it was for Darryl, I'm sure he was buoyed every step of the way by Davis's words of encouragement. And even if Davis hadn't said anything to him at all, Strawberry would have felt heartened just from having watched him in the '97 play-offs and the 1998 season, when he was again ripping the cover off the ball. For he could take comfort in seeing Davis handling his crisis with grace and that same sweet smile that Darryl had known for more than twenty years.

Barry Bonds

If August 23 had been an ordinary day in baseball, Barry Bonds surely would have been the sports world's headline grabber after blasting a home run off Florida's Kirt Ojala to become the first player in history to have four hundred homers and four hundred stolen bases in a career. But there weren't many ordinary days during the '98 season, and on the monumental day when Bonds hit "only" the twenty-sixth of his eventual thirty-seven homers for the year, McGwire smashed his fifty-third homer, Sosa his fiftieth and fifty-first, Griffey his forty-third, Mo Vaughn his forty-second, and Andres Galarraga became the first player to hit forty homers with two different teams in consecutive years. Bonds even had to share space with a young center fielder named Sayaka

Tsushima, who on this day became the first girl to play for a Far East Team in the Little League World Series.

Bonds himself downplayed his record-breaking day against the Marlins, saying he didn't feel his accomplishment compared to what Mark McGwire was doing. Yet considering that only three other players—Bonds's godfather, Willie Mays, his father, Bobby Bonds, and Andre Dawson—have even accumulated 300 steals and 300 bases, Bonds's achievement is tremendously impressive. Maybe it would have been more publicized if Bonds had been in his last season, rather than having many more years ahead to build on his record. It's unfinished business. Only thirty-four, Bonds, who finished the season with 411 homers and 445 stolen bases, will undoubtedly become the game's only 500-500 man! Now that is bound to make headlines. Along with his three MVP awards for Pittsburgh and San Francisco between 1990 and 1993, that will be his greatest achievement in a Hall of Fame career. The 400-400 mark is not only a remarkable stat but a true indicator of the type of player Bonds has been since breaking in with the Pirates thirteen years ago.

"Home-run guys" usually aren't also "stolen-base guys." There have been exceptions, like Willie Mays, the player Bonds emulated even more than he did his father, and whose NL record of reaching base fourteen consecutive times Bonds quietly broke last year. But for the most part sluggers haven't been runners. For Bonds, hitting with power and smart running go hand in hand. When a pitcher walks Bonds rather than chancing a pitch that he might drive out of the park, Bonds will want to impress upon that pitcher that a base on balls to him is the equivalent of a double. However, if a pitcher fears giving up a "two-base walk," he will often throw a pitch that Bonds can blast out of the ballpark. That is how Bonds became a three-time thirty-homers, thirty-steals man, and one of only three players to have had forty homers and forty steals in the same season.

Last May 28, Arizona manager Buck Showalter came up with a way to prevent Bonds from homering or stealing: With his team up 8–6 with two outs in the ninth, he had his pitcher Greg Olson intentionally walk the dangerous Bonds with the bases loaded! That was only the second time in history that a batter had been given an intentional pass with the bases jammed. I don't like that strategy, but it worked: The run scored, but Bonds remained at first when the next batter made the game's final out and Arizona escaped with an 8–7 victory. What Showalter did just proves how dangerous Bonds is considered, especially in clutch situations. That's why pitchers have walked him an average of 142 times in the last three years! As was Ted Williams, Bonds is sometimes unfairly criticized for accepting so many walks, but if he didn't have the discipline not to chase balls off the plate, it would detract from his effectiveness in hitting balls over the plate. In fact, pitchers would never see the need to challenge him in his zone.

What makes Bonds such a dangerous hitter is that his zone does include the ball just off the plate inside. As his former manager Jim Leyland pointed out to me, Bonds and Gary Sheffield are the only two guys in baseball today who have the ability to quickly adjust their hands and hit that inside pitch fair. And I think Bonds can do it better than anybody since Hank Aaron. From what I've seen, even Ken Griffey will hook that pitch foul. You don't see Bonds hook balls foul unless they are on the ground. And when he hits balls airborne to the right side they usually stay fair with serious consequences.

It's blasphemy not to call Ted Williams the best left fielder of all time, but I'd take Bonds. I will concede that Williams was the better hitter, especially for average—even though when Bonds also has put together a nineteen-year career he will have equaled or passed Williams in almost every other statistical category!

However, what makes Bonds my choice is that his running and fielding are vastly superior. He's not just an excellent base stealer, but always runs through the bag with the idea of taking an extra base (which is why he scores 120 runs each year) and always slides hard into fielders to break up double plays. In left field, his many Gold Gloves have been warranted. He can compensate for a mediocre throwing arm because nobody positions himself better according to who the hitters are and the nuances of their swings. Nobody has better anticipation. Here's a left-handed thrower who is willing to move toward the left-field line when necessary, although that means he'll have to attempt a harder backhand stop if the ball is hit to his left. Other left fielders won't take that chance, but Bonds is intelligent enough to play the percentages. It's amazing how many balls he gets to.

Bonds is such an exceptional ballplayer that you would think he would receive tremendous adulation from fans. But that has waned over the years. So what's the problem? Sure he's arrogant, someone whose attitude is "I don't care what you do, you can't stop me." But a lot of arrogant athletes are very popular with the fans, while Bonds is the one who is singled out for criticism. I think this is understandable. I think we as a society make certain demands of our heroes. We expect their appreciation of their feats to be commensurate with the magnitude of those feats. Maybe I'm delving too much into human nature, but I believe there is a deep-rooted feeling among people that athletes should show they enjoy what they are doing. We ask of Bonds, "Why should we enjoy what you're doing if you aren't enjoying it yourself?" Fans get annoyed that his egotism translates into saying derogatory things about his Giants manager, Dusty Baker. (Remember that quote: "Dusty Baker can kiss my ass!") Or into looking at a reporter as if he were scum for suggesting that he will feel more protected in the lineup once Jeff Kent returns from an injury—never mind that last year Kent became the first second baseman since Rogers Hornsby to drive in 120 runs in successive seasons. And when Bonds became the first 400-400 man, fans frowned on his quick dismissal of his achievement because they sensed it wasn't done with humility but with disregard. Bonds really understands the game of baseball, but there's no question that he'd make life easier on himself if he tried to understand the people who watch it. Then he could have been part of the celebration of the 1998 season instead of distancing himself from it.

Paul Molitor

It's the swing that I'll always remember about Paul Molitor. (You ain't got a thing if you ain't got that swing.) To be able to hit a baseball with any kind of power, a batter must have a trigger. Once his stance is set, he must pull the bat back before bringing it forward to make contact or he will be unable to generate power. And the quicker he takes it back the better. But Molitor had no trigger. His hands were perfectly still as he waited for the pitch and then they moved the bat forward from this set position. (Joe DiMaggio was the only other good hitter in memory who also did this.) How was he able to do this yet be an extraordinary hitter who racked up more than 950 extra-base hits in his illustrious twenty-one-year career? Molitor did it with hand speed and a whole lot of strength. You wouldn't think Molitor had a strong physique unless you got close to him. Then you'd be surprised by the unusual thickness in his back, chest, and arms. This guy is powerfully built.

In fact, Molitor had the power to hit far more than 234 home runs, but he preferred the purer approach of shooting line drives into the gaps, taking advantage of his speed to take him around the bases. Whenever a player combines base-running skills with hitting skills, especially if he's a gap hitter, then he really increases his value as an offensive player. Most baseball fans don't understand this concept; and a lot of baseball people don't get it either. They see that a guy's a good hitter and think that's enough; but Molitor always knew that he would be a much better offensive player if he made use of his razor-sharp base-running instincts. Here's a guy who always raced out of the batter's box, ran *through* bases instead of pulling up to them, and challenged outfielders' arms if he liked the odds of beating the ball to the next base. What tells you a lot about Molitor is that he is the only player in history to triple for his 3,000th hit. Not only didn't he stop at first to celebrate his milestone hit, he didn't stop at second either.

On August 28 last year, one day after Molitor doubled against Tampa Bay to pass Willie Mays and move into ninth place on the all-time hit list, Minnesota's designated hitter doubled again against the Devil Rays. It was the 600th double in the career of the St. Paul native. And it made him only the third player in history to record 3,000 hits, 600 doubles, and 500 stolen bases. You know what an accomplishment this is when you realize that the only two players who did it previously were Ty Cobb and Honus Wagner. Now that is select company. Obviously, the 3,000 hits was proof positive that Molitor had been a marvelous hitter for many years, but the other two stats better revealed the type of player he was: a batter and runner who was always hungry for the next base. He had remarkable instincts for when to stretch singles into doubles and doubles into triples, as was proven by how few times he was thrown out. Moreover, his stolen-base percentage was exceptional; in fact in the 1990s he was safe on 86 percent of his steals (166 of 193 attempts, including a perfect 32 for 32 in 1994 and 1995). When his bat was no longer in his hands, his legs were his weapons.

One of the many remarkable things about Molitor's career is how he steadily improved when other players might have seen their careers winding down. In fact nine of his twelve .300 seasons came after he passed thirty. And his two 100-RBI seasons came after he was thirty-seven. But those are just statistics. Perhaps many people didn't realize that he was already a splendid all-around player in his first few years with the Milwaukee Brewers. What little national attention the Brewers were accorded then was usually directed at popular future Hall of Famer Robin Yount, another player with diverse skills. And though Molitor was playing numerous positions and putting up big numbers as a leadoff hitter those few seasons he could escape injuries, it was generally assumed that he was a complement to Milwaukee's glamour player, not his equal. Who could believe that the small-market Brewers could have two future Hall of Famers in their lineup? But when

Molitor followed up a standout 1982 season with a brilliant showing in the Brewers' seven-game World Series defeat to St. Louis, including a record-setting five-for-five in the first game, there were indications that he was ready to break through into the public's eye and get his due.

However, his momentum was repeatedly interrupted by injuries. If anybody had told me back then that his body would hold up long enough for him to get three thousand hits, I would have laughed. Because the young Molitor had some real problems that made it difficult for him to suit up and play. In fact, he missed almost all of the 1984 season when he had ligaments replaced in his elbow; in 1986, he was on the disabled list three times. In all he would miss over five hundred games.

Oddly it was in 1987, when he played in only 118 games, that he finally emerged into the spotlight. It took a thrilling thirty-nine-game hit streak, the fifth best in history, to turn baseball fans' eyes toward Milwaukee. During the latter stages of that streak, he was baseball's biggest story. That he won over the fans was evident the next year, when they voted him the American League's starting second baseman for the All-Star Game although he'd played only one game at the position during the season.

Somewhere along the line you say, "Wow. This guy isn't just a very good player. He's a great player." That is what happened with Molitor in the late 1980s. Then in the 1990s, you find yourself revising your thinking again: "Hey, he isn't just a great player. He's a Hall of Fame player." In the nineties, Molitor had several more outstanding seasons with the Brewers before playing three years each with Toronto and Minnesota, coming home. He didn't seem to age. In his first year with the Blue Jays he got to play in his second World Series, twelve years after the one with Milwaukee. Although he'd been a DH all year, he played two games at third base and one at first base in Philadelphia and played excellent defense. And his bat was on fire. One of baseball's great clutch hitters, Molitor went 12-for-24 against Phillies pitching, with two doubles, two triples, two homers, ten runs, and eight RBIs in Toronto's six-game victory. All with the whole world watching. Molitor turned forty in his first year with Minnesota but still continued to produce, batting .341, driving in a career-high 113 runs, and becoming the first forty-year-old to have over 200 hits (a career-high 225). Nicknamed the "Igniter" early in his career, he now could have been called the "Finisher."

Molitor's foot and bat speed would slow down slightly, but in 1998 he confirmed that he could be a productive player for another few years. However, two months after matching the record that had been held by Cobb and Wagner for seventy years, and soon after he singled in his final at-bat of the year to move into eighth place for career hits, Molitor announced it was time to retire (although he carefully avoided that word at his press conference). A true professional, a man who has always exuded class, a great guy who has won awards for community service, a smart guy, Paul Molitor realized that there was no better time to hang it up. He had played his part in the one season that can never be equaled.

Derek Jeter, Nomar Garciaparra, and Alex Rodriguez

Talk about star power. A few years after the advent of the Three Tenors, the Three Shortstops made their first big splash. Just as Pavarotti, Domingo, and Carreras had done much to popularize opera with the masses, the equally dynamic trio of New York's Derek Jeter, Boston's Nomar Garciaparra, and Seattle's Alex Rodriguez would rekindle America's interest in baseball in the post-strike years. They were able to have such impact on a disgruntled public by injecting the sport with an exciting blend of youth, talent, and undeniable class.

The three young superstars are often talked about in the same breath, for obvious reasons. First of all, they became instant-impact players at early ages and at virtually the same time—Jeter at twenty-two and Rodriguez at twenty-one first played extensively in 1996, Garciaparra at twenty-four debuted in 1997. Second, they have other similar credentials: Jeter and Garciaparra were Rookies of the Year; Rodriguez was second to Juan Gonzalez in the MVP race in 1996, and Garciaparra and Jeter finished second and third to Gonzalez in 1998; all three have been All-Stars (with Rodriguez becoming the youngest All-Star shortstop in '96). Also: As is indicated by their many rave quotes about one another's play and personalities, they quickly formed a very public mutual admiration society—in fact, Jeter and Rodriguez have become the best of friends. Most significant, because there are three of them rather than just one groundbreaker—as was the case with Cal Ripken, Jr.—they have had the enormous effect of forever redefining the shortstop position. (Ozzie Smith changed the position also, but only defensively.) It's not just that they are tall for shortstops—Rodriguez and Jeter are six-feet-three and Garciaparra is six feet—but that they are all both excellent fielders and excellent power hitters. They have exhibited the range, grace, and creativity to rank just below Gold Glovers Omar Vizquel and Rey Ordoñez in the field, so in years past they wouldn't have been required to hit for average, much less power. Yet these three do both. Last year Jeter, who became the first Yankee shortstop since Phil Rizzuto in 1950 to collect 200 hits, batted .324, Garciaparra .323, and Rodriguez .310. And they had pop in their bats: Third-place hitter Rodriguez drove in 124 runs, cleanup hitter Garciaparra had 122 RBIs, and Jeter knocked in 84 from the second spot in the order. Only once in a blue moon is an excellent-fielding shortstop associated with the long ball—again, the six-four Cal Ripken, Jr., was an anomaly—yet consider that last year all three shortstops hit milestone home runs:

- On August 29, in an 11–6 victory over the Mariners that resulted in the Yankees' clinching a postseason spot the earliest in their history, Jeter made a leaping catch, scored four runs, and had three hits, including his seventeenth homer, to set the team record for shortstops. He would increase his new record to nineteen homers by season's end.

- On September 2, Garciaparra hit a ninth-inning grand slam to give the Red Sox a 7–3 win over the Mariners and become only the fifth player to have thirty homers in his first two years in the majors. He would finish the season with thirty-five homers, five more than his rookie total.

- On September 19, Rodriguez belted his fortieth homer of the year in Seattle's 5–3 road loss to Anaheim to become the third player, following Jose Canseco and Barry Bonds, and the first infielder to have forty homers and forty stolen bases in a season. This was his biggest achievement of 1998, but on the twenty-second, he would smash his forty-first homer to break Rico Petrocelli's 1969 record for American League shortstops, and would go on to hit forty-two homers and steal forty-six bases.

Rodriguez and Garciaparra are frightening to pitch to because they have the long arms to give them exceptional plate coverage and the power to drive an outside pitch over the fence the other way. Rodriguez, in particular, has extraordinary power to right-center, and it boggles the mind when you see him drill the ball 425 feet that way and then remember that he's also a fine-fielding shortstop. Jeter has an inside-out swing that enables him to go the other way on an inside pitch but rarely does he hit any ball over the fence the opposite way. Yet, oddly enough, he jolted one ball out to right at Yankee Stadium early in the season that probably outdistanced anything Rodriguez and Garciaparra hit that way all year. Knowing that I don't concede that a tightly wrapped ball is the reason for so many homers in the majors, Joe Torre told me that Jeter's mammoth opposite-field drive into the upper deck in right was proof that the little white rat was wrapped tighter than a pro wrestler's corset.

I suppose if you were drafting a fantasy-league ball team, Alex Rodriguez would be the shortstop you'd pick first because of his combination of power, speed, and average—he was the third youngest to win a batting title when he batted .358 in 1996, and everyone expects him to repeat. The complete package, he is projected to become, if he's not already, the best player in baseball. However, right now, according to no less an authority than Jim Kaat, Nomar Garciaparra is baseball's best all-around shortstop. He isn't the base stealer Rodriguez (or Jeter) is, but if the young Californian hadn't missed three weeks last year almost all of his stats (his least favorite subject) would have equaled or bettered the young Mariner's extraordinary offensive numbers. Plus he has an edge over Rodriguez in the field.

Perhaps their power gives Rodriguez and Garciaparra a slight edge over Jeter with the bat, but I rate him the superior fielder. They don't come in on the ball as well as Jeter, nor do they have his range. For instance, Jeter goes into the hole better than anyone in the league, including Vizquel. Watch how he plants his foot and throws out batters with a strong, accurate arm. Garciaparra (who made a sensational play in the hole in the play-offs) and Rodriguez make this play, too, but not with the consistency of Jeter. Even better is how Jeter goes to his left. If you're in the park on this play, you might hear teammates of the batter yell from the dugout for grounders to stay down because they know shortstops usually need the ball to come up to make a clean play. But Jeter is the rare shortstop who will stay down with the ball, pick it up, and throw across his body to make the play. It's an extraordinary talent. I also like his smarts. For instance, last year he seemed keenly aware that his second baseman Chuck Knoblauch was having throwing problems, so Jeter always made sure to get the ball to him on double plays quickly enough for him to have time to make an easy pivot and throw.

What Jeter does on the double-play balls reveals the surprising maturity about the game that all three of these young shortstops possess. Throughout their brief careers, we've heard their managers, coaches, and veteran teammates expound on how they can't believe these guys play and act like they've been in the big leagues for years. The priority for most young players is image. I remember years ago when Mets rookie Gregg Jefferies was slightly miffed with me for revealing on the air that he was at least two inches shorter than the five feet ten inches that he was said to be in the media guide because, as the young bachelor told me, "there are a lot of women who watch the game." (Baseball lover President Nixon told me, "Why, if Jefferies is five-ten then Dukakis is six feet tall.") Jeter, who the joke goes, leads the league in proposals from fans, Rodriguez, and Garciaparra don't have such considerations. They let "image" take care of itself and concentrate on playing and winning. They have the correct priorities, know their responsibilities on the field and in the clubhouse. Jeter, whose father is black and mother white, has proved to be the ideal person to stick dead center into a clubhouse with players of all colors and nationalities. Even at his tender age, players of all ilks have gravitated toward him, which is why he is being groomed to be a future Yankee captain. It would already be a suitable role for Jeter, who has the poise and toughness to handle such a job, even though former Yankee captain Graig Nettles, when given the title, wondered, "What does this mean—that I'll get to call the coin toss?"

What has really impressed everybody about the Three Shortstops is that despite their tremendous success and extreme popularity, they have exhibited both a love for the game of baseball and a respect for its past players and traditions. When you hear Jeter talk about growing up (in New Jersey and Michigan) and loving the New York Yankees, you know how thrilled he is to be wearing pinstripes and playing for fans in hallowed Yankee Stadium. You know he believes he has been entrusted to carry on the great tradition of his team and that he takes that responsibility very seriously. One can appreciate his knowledge of baseball history when he expresses his gratitude to Jackie Robinson for paving the way for all the black players who have followed him into the majors. But when he goes on to say that Rachel Robinson "had just as much a role as he did, maybe even bigger," you realize just how real is his passion for the sport and all the people who came before him. And the other two players have the same respect for the game.

In fact, Alex Rodriguez grew up watching Mets games and was such a fan of Keith Hernandez that he now wears number 17 to honor his idol. I think that his choice of a favorite player indicated an early appreciation for players who were as adept with the glove as they were with the bat. That's the type of player Rodriguez has worked tirelessly to become.

Because they were fans of the game, all three shortstops have a remarkable dedication to it. That's why Rodriguez is famous for taking extra fielding practice. That's why Jeter puts past accomplishments aside and says honestly, "In baseball, until you hit one thousand and have no errors, you'll always have something to work on." That's why Bob Ryan of *The Boston Globe* can write, "Many a ballplayer will look you squarely in the eye and tell you how he's not about the stats or the money, that the only thing he cares about is the final outcome, even as insincerity oozes from every pore—and then there is Nomar Garciaparra, [who] when [he] says he couldn't tell you his stats is telling the gospel truth."

Jeter, Rodriguez, and Garciaparra recognize their vital

roles in helping baseball reclaim its spot as America's pastime as it heads into the twenty-first century. They are the leaders of an exciting crop of young players that includes Kerry Wood, Ben Grieve, Vladimir Guerrero, Ugueth Urbina, Todd Helton, J. D. Drew, Scott Rolen, and Andruw Jones. Of being regarded as saviors, Rodriguez (in *Inside Sports*) says candidly, "I think being post-strike players has a lot to do with the labels they put on us. Saying that we're going to save the game—that's a lot of pressure for a young guy. I think you just have to go out and be the best person you can be, on and off the field, and let the chips fall where they may."

Jeter concurs. "Alex and I have talked about this before, and what we've decided is, what you see is what you get. We're not going to try and go out and act a certain way—we're going to act as we've always acted. If people want to see us *that* way, I have no problem with that."

Garciaparra pretty much sums it up: "I get the strong feeling that there are a lot of players in our generation who accept the responsibility for returning baseball to its rightful spot as the most popular sport. I watch Jeter and Rodriguez and many others, and I know that they feel the way I do—that the players before us made this a great game, and that we respect what we have been given."

It's clear: Not only has the shortstop position blossomed because of these three young sensations, but under the influence of such first-class baseball citizens, the sport itself is in good hands.

Jim Abbott

I didn't get to see Jim Abbott pitch in 1998, but like most people who hoped for the one-time star left-hander to have success with his September comeback, I made sure to find out the outcome of each of his starts. It turned out to be the same outcome each time. Beginning with his first start of the season and first appearance in the majors since 1996, Abbott won five straight times: 5-0. In the "perfect" season, you can't get much more perfect than that.

Five wins may not seem like a whole lot, especially when pitching in the final month for a team not in pennant contention, but how Abbott must have cherished each of those wins, not even caring that his ERA was a bit high. He remembers '96, when his record was a disastrous 2-18 and he just couldn't get a break that would give him a cheap victory. (When the Angels optioned him that August to Vancouver, it marked the first time that the former University of Michigan and Olympic star had pitched in the minors.) In 1997, Abbott got no wins at all. The whole year was spent at home with his wife and baby daughter while he contemplated whether he still had a career in baseball. Abbott decided he loved the game too much not to give it one more try and in late May signed a minor league contract with the pitching-depleted White Sox. He obligingly rode the buses until Chicago expanded its roster in September, and he was relieved to see manager Jerry Manuel immediately pencil him into his five-man rotation. And from out of the blue Abbott became one of the nicest stories of the year.

I was more surprised by Abbott's precipitous decline in 1996 than by his comeback last season. I was stunned by how quickly he went south. I realized that he hadn't been the effective pitcher he'd been in his early years with the Angels, or the one who no-hit the Indians while pitching for the Yankees in 1993. But his stuff was still too good for him to suddenly have an astronomical 7.48 ERA in 1996. His descent was meteoric. And it was upsetting because of who Abbott was, someone who had such desire to pitch that he learned how to field his position despite having been born with a withered right hand. He was a tremendous inspiration to all physically challenged athletes (and nonathletes as well), and such a nice person that people jested that they saw a halo over him when he pitched for the Angels.

However, when a pitcher's best pitch is an inside pitch, he's in big trouble if that pitch stops being effective. Because that pitch can be hit a long way. Sure enough, Abbott's career was in big trouble after his bread-and-butter pitch, a cut fastball that came in to right-handed batters (the same pitch that Yankee lefty Andy Pettitte relies on), lost its velocity and bite, but Abbott has been willing to change his style. "I know my fastball isn't what it used to be," he said after some early-September success, "but I still like to use it, nick the corners, throw it where they don't expect it, just to try to stay aggressive. The key is control. I've got to get my pitches over the plate." In truth, the jury is still out on whether he can get his pitches over the plate and get batters out for a full season. But for now, Abbott, who signed a contract for 1999 with Milwaukee, is just thrilled to be back in the big leagues. "I can't believe I'm back here again," he says, beaming. "It feels so good to be here. I'm going to enjoy this while I can." How can you not root for someone with that attitude?

Randy Johnson

"I can't walk on water," Randy Johnson once insisted, "I can't part the Red Sea." But September 7, the Cincinnati players doubted those words were true because Johnson, figuratively speaking, took apart the Reds easily. Fourteen befuddled batters went down on strikes in the Reds' 1–0 loss to the Houston Astros' new ace, including three in a row after he bore down with a man on third and no outs in the eighth inning. This was after he dramatically struck out the side in the fifth inning, the only other time the Reds threatened. The more than forty thousand awed fans in the Astrodome cheered louder with each strike; and Houston manager Larry Dierker admitted he got chills watching the animated Johnson do what he does best. "I don't like to go for strikeouts," Johnson would say later, "but the game was on the line and I went for it."

This was the eighteenth time in 1998 and the fifth time in eight starts since Houston acquired him from the generous Seattle Mariners on July 31 that the Big Unit had a double-digit strikeout total. Most significant, Johnson, three days shy of his thirty-fifth birthday, joined Nolan Ryan as the only pitchers in history to strike out at least ten batters in one hundred games!

The six-hitter was the imposing left-hander's fourth shutout in the four starts he would get during the regular season in front of the delighted and vocal fans at the Astrodome. It improved his record to 7-1 for his new team. After three more starts, including his 101st and 102nd double-digit strikeout games, Johnson's final record with Houston would be an extraordinary 10-1 with a 1.28 ERA and 116 strikeouts in 84⅓ innings to finish with a career-high 329 K's. After struggling with the Mariners for four months, he rebounded with the strongest audition possible for an enormous free-agent contract after the season. He subsequently settled with the Arizona Diamondbacks.

I wasn't surprised by how well Johnson did in the National League. But I was surprised at how ineffective he was with the Mariners. In the previous five years with Seattle, Johnson had gone 75-20. He was 18-2 in 1995, 5-0 in 1996, and 20-4 in 1997; and while compiling a 43-6 record over those three years, his ERA was only 2.54, and he fanned 670 batters in 484⅔ innings. Then in '98, Johnson's record with Seattle dipped to 9-10, his ERA ballooned to 4.33, and he gave up only one less hit while pitching 53 fewer innings than in 1997. The question on everybody's mind was whether he was hurting again. In 1996, a herniated disk in his back limited him to just eight starts and required surgery even before the season ended. Since then everyone has worried about his back, as well as his arm. In Houston, he proved that his body was sound.

What went wrong with Johnson in Seattle was probably related to his not being offered a new contract by the team he'd pitched for since the early part of 1989. Mariners president Chuck Armstrong swore to the media that he had no plans to trade his star pitcher and crowd favorite, but every time Johnson pitched I know he wondered if it was his last outing with the team. He knew that with free agency on the horizon, his contract demands would be prohibitive to a team that would have to make beyond-lucrative offers to keep Ken Griffey, Jr., and Alex Rodriguez, who would both be free agents in a couple of years. Knowing that he was gone, how could Johnson or any other player put forth his best effort, from a human standpoint, a contractual standpoint, or a commonsense standpoint? How could he give the fan his money's worth?

I think the Players Association and ownership should look hard at those uncomfortable situations when a player's team has left him dangling, because his integrity will be challenged if he isn't up to par. As his bad showings mounted, Johnson was criticized by the media for not giving 100 percent. And he even got into one of those locker-room pushing and shoving matches with his teammate David Segui. Perhaps it was the anger he felt after that tiff that propelled him the next day to throw his first shutout of the year and strike out fifteen batters against Anaheim. Johnson has always thrived on emotion, yet that was one of the few games he had with the Mariners where he allowed himself to show any. While he admitted that not knowing his status with the team was a distraction, he told the press that he deeply resented the insinuations that he didn't care about his efforts, or wasn't trying or working just as hard in '98 as he had in his more successful years. However, he did hint that at the root of his problems was his lack of enjoyment pitching for a team that didn't want him anymore. "My problem is not mechanical, it's between the ears," he said. "If you're not having fun at what you do, that might reflect a little bit on how you perform."

After being traded to postseason-bound Houston, Johnson had his Astros cap screwed on tight and he was having fun again. Which was bad news for opposing batters. At times last season, National League batters, including Mark McGwire in a couple of classic battles, were completely overmatched by Johnson. It reminded me of those times in the Little League when one team's manager sends a towering, adult-looking ringer to the mound to face cowering, four-foot-five twelve-year-olds.

I don't know if I've ever seen a pitcher more fearsome than Randy Johnson. He jokes: "I sometimes think my own teammates are intimidated by me." The former basketball player is so tall and has such extension that it seems to the hitter that the ball is on top of him in a flash. Batters can't dig in because he loves to throw inside, and what's worse is that he enjoys exhibiting an occasional touch of wildness. He wants to maintain the reputation for being conveniently wild because he knows the effect that has on batters. Believe me that when they must face Johnson in a game, they do remember the images of John Kruk comically quaking in his shoes at the '93 All-Star Game after a Johnson pitch flew over his head; left-handed Larry Walker batting right-handed against Johnson in the '97 All-Star Game as a compliment to his scary pal; and hard sliders that have gone up and in to Kenny Lofton, his personal favorite target. "[He's] been throwing at me since '92," protests Lofton. "A lot of guys laugh about it, but it's not funny."

Intimidation is just one more weapon in Johnson's arsenal. He already has two wicked pitches. First there is his frightening 96-mph high fastball. Then there is Johnson's signature pitch, a sweeping slider. Right-handed batters have a difficult time reading the spin on the slider, because it's bigger than the more conventional and tightly wrapped "dime" and more loosely wrapped "quarter" spins. The slider starts so far outside that batters give up on it early, thinking it will be called a ball, but it will suddenly sweep over the corner for a called strike. When both Johnson's fastball and slider are working, as they were after he came to Houston, he is nearly unhittable.

The July 31 trade of Johnson to Houston was a shock, especially because all Mariners general manager Woody Woodward received in return were three minor leaguers who weren't even considered top prospects. It had been speculated that the Cleveland Indians were the team that would acquire Johnson in order to have a dominating left-handed starter to go against New York in the play-offs. The

Yankees were thrilled that Johnson was dealt to the Astros instead because Johnson was the one pitcher in baseball they really feared could turn a short series around against them. However, the thought of playing against the Astros in the World Series now was worrisome to the Yankees. In fact, when the trade was made and Johnson returned to form, the Astros became the team no one wanted to play in the postseason. A unique pitcher, Randy Johnson had the talent and presence to terrify entire organizations.

Roger Maris

It was great television. For one of my few times as a broadcaster, I couldn't take my eyes off the monitor. I didn't want to. And I knew viewers at home were riveted as well. We saw Mark McGwire, after hitting his record-breaking sixty-second homer of the season off the Cubs' Steve Trachsel, climb into the box seats to the left of the first-base dugout as if he were a soldier leaving a bunker. Then he swiftly ran up the steps to hug the grown children of Roger Maris, a spontaneous, heartfelt gesture that both linked him with and paid great tribute to the special man whose record had lasted thirty-seven years. Before the packed crowd at Busch Stadium and millions of people at home watching the FOX broadcast, they were sharing a private moment. McGwire's classy overture reaffirmed in the minds of the Marises that if Roger's record had to be broken, it was done by the right person.

So many thoughts flashed through my head as I watched this truly emotional scene unfold. For one thing, I was thinking of how McGwire's record-breaker was cause for him to celebrate, though he was sensitively tempering his personal joy to acknowledge Maris and his family. And I thought about how when Roger ended his lonely quest to break Babe Ruth's record on the final day of the 1961 season—sending a Tracy Stallard fastball into the right-field stands at Yankee Stadium on October 1, 1961, two years to the day before McGwire was born—he felt relief rather than a desire to celebrate. A nightmare had ended, and this shy man even had to be coaxed out of the dugout to tip his hat. I was also thinking of how much Maris's sons, whom I knew as young boys, looked like their father, down to the crewcuts. Most of all I was thinking about how receptive the entire Maris family had been to McGwire and Sammy Sosa throughout the season, although it became increasingly clear that their dad would lose the record that kept his name alive and was his most impressive credential for Hall of Fame consideration. They had not even a trace of spitefulness. That is how Roger would have reacted. Had cancer not taken his life in 1985 at the early age of fifty-one, he too would have rooted for McGwire to pass him by. I know my friend would have attended the game, especially in St. Louis, where he played his final and happiest two years in baseball. He would have finally celebrated.

The Cardinals played against Roger in the 1964 World Series, yet when he showed up at our spring training camp in 1967, having been acquired for Charlie Smith, we were unprepared for the type of person he was. He had none of the affectations that one might expect from the famous Number 9, who had spent the previous seven seasons in New York, snagged MVP awards in 1960 and 1961, played in five World Series, and had claimed baseball's most glamorous record. I would drive to the ballpark with him every day, frequently go with him to restaurants, and spend a lot of time with him, as well as his wife, Pat—with whom I still exchange Christmas cards—and their six kids. Of course I was impressed that he held the homer record, but I never thought about that when we were together. Roger wouldn't allow you to feel any awe toward him because of what he had achieved. So all I saw was a nice, quiet man from Fargo, North Dakota, as plain and genuine as anybody you'd ever meet. His smile as a grown man was that of a young boy. What struck us all was that he had the carriage of a winner on and off the field. Had he gotten it as a Yankee? Or further back, when he was a baseball and high-school football star who set the still-standing North Dakota record with five TDs in a game? In any case, he brought that winning attitude from New York to St. Louis, and it's no coincidence that we made it to the World Series in both years he manned right field for us. Maris ended up playing in seven World Series in nine seasons, and winning four rings—nobody played in or won as many World Series as Maris during the sixties.

There are great players who aren't winners and winners who aren't great players, but he was a winner and a great player. He was no longer a consistent power hitter at this time but he still had that graceful left-handed swing. What surprised us most were his ancillary skills. We had no idea what a tremendous all-around ballplayer he was. As the Hall of Fame voters don't seem to realize, he was a superb outfielder, had a very strong arm, could run the bases, and took guys out on double plays with hard slides. Such a force in football that he was courted by Bud Wilkinson of Oklahoma, Roger had a solid build, with a big rear and big thighs, and he was like a battering ram when he came into a base. He was a star known for his bat yet was willing to put his aging body on the line for the team. His love of contact was contagious to the younger players.

Roger was surely inspirational and helpful to me. One time in Pittsburgh, I was facing Steve Blass with men on second and third. I usually hit Blass well but this time I managed only to trickle the ball back to the box on a checked swing. Blass looked the runners back and easily threw me out. I was so livid that I stormed out of the dugout and past the rancid bathroom and back down the tunnel, which at Forbes Field was like a catacomb. Holding in my emotions wasn't my strong suit when I was a young player, and I was determined to break my bat. So I started pounding it against the walls and the floor. I had much better swings at the cement than I had against Blass. But it was to no avail. I just couldn't break it. I was fuming. Then I looked up and saw that Roger had followed me in. He smiled as he asked me, "What do you think would happen to this team if you got hurt?" It was as if somebody had pulled a shade up and the light came in. I said, "I've never really thought about that before." "Well, isn't it time you started thinking along those lines?" he asked, before making his point: "Your value to this team is a helluva lot more than what you do in one at-bat." He wasn't berating me, just letting me know that he understood. Only Kenny Boyer had ever said something like that to me before, and, looking back at my career, I know that his saying that was one of the major reasons I was able to mature as I did. When Roger said something, it had an impact.

Everyone on the team looked up to Roger and was aware that he was a special person. To be invited to dinner with him was a real treat. Roger had developed a love for crabmeat and would usually take other players to restaurants that served it. (In fact he and his fast friend Mike Shannon once ordered Dungeness crab to be delivered to them before our plane took off so they could feast on that while the rest of us were stuck with regular airplane fare.) One time Roger asked Hal Woodeshick, a relief pitcher with nasty stuff, to go with him to a restaurant in Philadelphia. Woody was an impressionable guy, and that dinner he had with Roger was all he could talk about for three days. He'd wax euphoric: "Roger and I went out to eat the other night. We had some crab. Oh, was it good!" It got to the point where we'd send the clubhouse guy or anybody else we could find over to him to say, "I heard you went out to eat with Roger." And Woody would go into his story again, not missing any details. He must have told that story thirty times, each time as though it were the first time.

The restaurant that received rave reviews from Roger was the Spindle Top in New York City. Roger told us so many times what a great restaurant it was that we couldn't wait until we finally traveled to the Big Apple to play the Mets and could go there with him. But when we arrived in New York, Roger informed us, "I'm not going." "Why not?" I asked. "You mean to tell me that you're not going to your favorite restaurant in the whole country?" He answered, "I never go out in New York anymore." The sad truth was that Roger's miserable experiences while eating out in public in New York in 1961 and subsequent years would keep him a prisoner in the hotel. He just couldn't bear to relive those moments when fans or reporters saw him dining out in New York. He made no bones about it: He hated New York. Roger would never talk to me or anyone else about breaking Ruth's record, unless he talked about the bad things he endured. His negative memories included losing his hair in patches due to the constant haranguing by some reporters, the hounding by mercenary autograph seekers, and Commissioner Ford Frick's vocal assertion that Maris's record deserved an asterisk by it unless he broke the record of Frick's friend in the 154 games the Babe played in 1927. "As a ballplayer, I would be delighted to do it again," Maris remarked after setting the new record. "[But] as an individual, I doubt if I could possibly go through it again." He told me, "Fans have asked for my autograph at every conceivable place—once at a urinal, once at mass." Boy, does that run the gamut.

The New York fans for the most part pulled for longtime Yankee Mickey Mantle to break Ruth's record over the outfielder who had played with the Kansas City A's just two years before. But at Yankee Stadium they were generally civil to Maris in '61 and cheered for him to pass Ruth once it was clear in early September that Mantle wasn't going to do it. (Mantle suffered a hip injury, was infected by a dirty needle while receiving treatment from a quack doctor, and settled for fifty-four homers.) Ironically, the fans in New York and on the road lavished attention on him when he dared to wander out into public yet were indifferent to him at the ballpark, as is evident from the thousands of empty seats for the game in which Ruth's record fell. It was in the spring of 1962, when the media got on Maris for demanding a hefty pay increase, that the fans really began to cruelly boo Maris, as they had done Mantle for years, every time he struck out. Maris replaced Mantle as Peck's Bad Boy in the city. They would continue to cheer Mantle and attack Maris until Roger was pretty much chased out of town. If he hadn't been traded after the 1966 season, he would have retired then.

Worse than the fans were some of the media. "Mickey and I were the best of friends," Roger would tell me. "We roomed together, we ate together, we'd walk to the ballpark together. Yet the press would try to make it seem like we were bitter rivals to stir up the fans against me. For instance, when we both had around fifty homers, there was the headline 'Maris jealous of Mantle.' And I'm asking, 'Where do these guys come up with these things? Don't they have to substantiate a story before they put it in print?' "

The press wrote about how Roger had an attitude and was testy whenever he did an interview. What I see when I look at films of his press interviews as he neared the home-run record is a guy who is patiently trying to answer every question. He is not having any fun and he is swallowing a lot, which is a sign to me that he felt nervous and out of place. He was trying to be honest, but his uneasy manner was the result of his not being skilled in this type of communication. How Maris would have loved to have been protected from the media and not be subjected to eternal interviews after every game, whether a home run was hit or not. Of course, in those days no one was prepared for a media onslaught, so perhaps the Yankees organization of that time should be forgiven for allowing Maris to be thrown to the lions. Then again, if Maris had watched how well the Cards and Cubs orchestrated press conferences for McGwire and Sosa in 1998, I think he would have felt envy. "Damn it!" he might have exclaimed. "Why weren't the Yankees smart enough to do that for me?"

Roger was the antithesis of a publicity hound. He was the type who wanted to be at home with his wife and kids rather than calling even more attention to himself by doing personal interviews. But he felt it was his burden to bear, what was expected of the player who was chasing a record that was part of the American psyche. That he was trying to go one up on the immortal Babe Ruth, in New York yet, was the worst thing that could have happened to him. He was as ill suited to play in the media capital as Mickey Mantle was in the 1950s after he arrived from Commerce, Oklahoma. Quite simply, Maris, too, became a victim of culture shock.

I know that Roger had great pride in being the first

man to hit sixty-one home runs in a season. He once said, too humbly, "I may not be a great man, but I damn well want to break the record." Though he rarely talked about his feat, I have no doubt that it was a great source of pride, particularly because it meant so much to his family and to all the citizens of Fargo, the location of the Roger Maris Museum. But having known Roger well, I do believe that he would have preferred to have hit the sixty-one homers in a place like Fargo. And I think he would not have told anyone until the record-breaker went sailing over the fence.

Manny Ramirez

The McGwire-Sosa home-run race was so embraced by the public that it seemed like many other stars, their pride suffering, tried to come up with ways to draw attention to their own longball talents. Alex Rodriguez became the first infielder to hit forty homers and steal forty bases in a season; Barry Bonds became baseball's first four hundred homer, four hundred stolen-base man for a career; Jose Canseco set the record for homers by a Hispanic player; Andres Galarraga became the first major leaguer to have back-to-back forty-homer seasons on two different teams. And Cleveland outfielder Manny Ramirez was able to make a lasting impression by going on a record-tying home-run tear in mid-September. On the fifteenth, the twenty-six-year-old Dominican exploded with his thirty-eighth, thirty-ninth, and fortieth homers in a 7–5 victory over Toronto. On the sixteenth, when the Indians clinched their fourth AL Central title in a row with an 8–4 home victory over Minnesota, Ramirez tied a major league record by going deep in his fourth consecutive at-bat and later clubbed his forty-second round-tripper to tie the record of five homers in two games. He would homer in his next game to tie another record—the last of six previous players to have six homers in three games was my teammate Mike Schmidt in 1976. And after one homerless game, Manny was back for more history, blasting his forty-fourth and forty-fifth homers in a loss to Kansas City. (Jose Rosado was so perturbed after yielding a three-run homer to Ramirez in the first inning that he and catcher Mike Sweeney engaged in fisticuffs in the dugout.) As often as McGwire and Sosa homered during the season, and at times it seemed like a daily occurrence, they never hit them at this pace. In fact, in major league history, only mammoth Frank Howard, who did it twice for the Washington Senators in 1968, had ever hit eight homers in five games before. And this wasn't just a hot streak in a vacuum. In the eighty-five games after June 15, Ramirez belted thirty-three homers and drove in ninety-seven runs! If Ramirez had done this to open the season, the media might have followed him around instead of McGwire.

Since Ramirez broke into the majors in 1993, he has been one of the most interesting hitters to watch. In fact, if I were a young right-handed batter, I might study him (or Nomar Garciaparra) because he truly has excellent form, with no wasted motions. As Ted Williams preached,

Ramirez has a grip so loose on the bat that you could knock it out of his hands with a slight tap. He maintains that grip until he makes contact. It used to be the case that left-handed batters were low-ball hitters and right-handed batters were high-ball hitters, but Ramirez is one of the rapidly growing new breed of low-ball-hitting right-handed power hitters who have emerged in the last dozen years. When he sees a ball from his mid-thigh to the top of his knee, he uncoils like a snake and destroys those pitches. Unlike most power hitters, he doesn't try to jerk anything over the fence but goes with the pitch. He goes the other way with an awful lot of power. Rather than being a thinking hitter, he pretty much hits what he sees with a rare explosiveness. But, most important, he's one of the young sluggers who benefits from the refusal of young AL pitchers to throw inside.

As the Cleveland fans attest, Ramirez has established himself as one of the brightest young stars in the game. His stats have been consistently impressive, and although he dipped to .294 last year after three successive years over .300, his power numbers were by far the best of his career. In any other year, a player who smashed 45 homers and drove in 145 RBIs would be a front-runner in the MVP race, but in 1998 it was only good enough to give him also-ran status.

I'm sure the Indians would be satisfied if Ramirez duplicated last season's offensive numbers in future years. But manager Mike Hargrove continues to challenge him to become a better all-around player. Certainly Manny's base running and outfield play need makeovers, and he can't go on a zany daytime talk show to get them. He is poor in both areas, yet I've sensed that he thinks his production with the bat gives him an exemption from having to make the effort to improve in these less glamorous parts of the game. I haven't yet seen in Ramirez the desire and dedication that are necessary for him become a multidimensional player. I hope he proves me wrong because the way he swings the bat, any improvement in the rest of his game will elevate him from All-Star to superstar in time for the twenty-first century.

Cal Ripken, Jr.

I wouldn't be surprised if during the last four or five years Rodney Dangerfield or some other standup comic who specialized in self-deprecating humor said the line "I'm such a loser that I finally got a ticket to see the Orioles and Cal Ripken didn't play." Who would have suspected that the fans who were present at Camden Yards on September 30, when Ripken's amazing iron-man playing streak ended after 2,632 games, would be delighted that they chose to attend the first game since May 29, 1982, that he sat out? They felt like winners because they realized they were present as history was being made, even though this was the rare time history was made when nothing happened, when somebody *didn't* do something. Following the stunning announcement that rookie Ryan Minor would be starting at third base for Baltimore, many stumbled to the souvenir stands to snap up scorecards and other souvenirs that would be proof of their whereabouts on this night. Meanwhile fans at home who had been to the park the previous day furiously searched through their pockets and garbage bins for the suddenly valuable stubs from the last game of Ripken's streak.

Only O's manager Ray Miller, who informed Minor that he was about to become an answer to a trivia question, and Brady Anderson knew of Ripken's decision to sit out the game, although many at the park became suspicious that something was up when Ripken skipped his ritualistic pregame throwing on the sidelines. Undoubtedly Ripken could have created a frenetic media event by announcing he would sit out a particular game a week or two in advance. But he kept secret his decision to sit on the bench during the Orioles' final home game of the year, taking the same low-key approach toward the end of the streak as he always had displayed toward the streak itself. It was a choice that confirmed he really believed what he had been saying all along, that he was uncomfortable because the streak brought him so much attention that the team itself was being overlooked by the fans and the media. He knew that when a reporter had the opportunity to ask him only one question, he would inquire about The Streak rather than about what Ripken thought of the Orioles' pennant chances.

Although I always look forward to seeing Ripken take the field, I think his decision to end the streak was belated. I agree with him that his streak had become a distraction to his teammates—just as I think Mark McGwire's Cardinals teammates last year performed far below their potentials because of the distractions caused by the home-run chase. Also, because Ray Miller knew it had to be strictly Ripken's call about ending the streak, he couldn't rest his aging player even if he knew it would benefit both the player and the team. His hands were tied. Although Ripken passed Brooks Robinson as Baltimore's all-time hits leader on August 21, he suffered through what was by far the worst offensive year of his career and was criticized in the press for stubbornly refusing to take a day off. If it weren't for the fact that the end of the streak became such a cause for celebration, Ripken would have been one of the disappointing stories of the season instead of one of the best.

What Ripken achieved during his Streak is such a phenomenal example of persistence and courage. If his sitting down was belated, his motives to play every day year after year haven't been in question since 1994. He came across as being unselfish when he was still short of Lou Gehrig's record 2,130 games in a row yet stated he would remain on strike even if baseball resumed with replacement players. (The point became moot when Baltimore owner Peter Angelos said he wouldn't go against the players' union and field minor leaguers.) I remember when Gehrig loyalists accused Ripken of playing every day simply to displace their idol in the record book, but as Ripken was modestly telling the world that "Gehrig was a better player than me," he passed the Yankee great on September 6, 1995, and, like the Energizer Bunny, kept on going and going.

Three years and 502 games later, no one could still think that beating Gehrig had been an obsession. Rather than the record, it was his reputation that he wanted to establish: "I want people to say [about me]," he explained, "[that] they can't keep him out of the lineup." Fans loved him even when they were angry at the rest of the baseball population in 1995, because, like them, he got up and went to his job every day and took pride in his work. In 1995, the legendary *Washington Post* writer Shirley Povich (who died just two months before the *Los Angeles Times's* award-winning Jim Murray last year) ably explained Ripken's impact:

> Organized baseball got luckier than it deserved in the emergence of Ripken as savior of much of the game's charms. In a year when major league baseball has few friends, when boycott is in the air and attendance is down 20 percent . . . when the players struck and walked out on the owners and, with both factions united only in their public-be-damned stance, Ripken came riding in from the east as the Peace Maker who brings fans back to the game.

It would have been beyond foolhardy for Ripken or any other young player to formulate a plan to break a consecutive-game playing streak, especially one over two thousand games long. Even if his various managers would be willing to play him every game for fourteen or fifteen years, what are the chances that he wouldn't be injured somewhere along the line? I'd say that most ballplayers have something wrong with them physically about 40 percent of the time, and that would be higher for an everyday shortstop, which Ripken was until the 1997 season. And so many other things can go wrong over such a long period of time. Ironically, last year Mexican League iron-man Gerardo Sanchez had his streak stopped after 1,415 games not because of an injury but because his flight was canceled when smoke from a nearby forest blaze inundated the airport. Talk about "burnout." That Ripken always got to the park on time and played despite several injuries and obvious fatigue is a testament to such figures as former manager Earl Weaver and Frank Robinson, whose influence on the organization has been profound. However, I'd say that both Ripken's toughness and his work ethic can be traced to the lifelong influence of Cal Ripken, Sr., who coached and managed his son as an Oriole.

Tom McGraw, the hitting instructor for Houston, told me a story about Cal Ripken, Sr. Apparently he was tilling the soil with some farm instrument when it bounced up and laid his head open right across the forehead. It would require about fifteen stitches, but at the time, he went to his house, simply butterflied it with needle and thread, and went back to his business. Only after he had finished his chore did he go to the doctor. The doctor was aghast when he saw him and implored, "Cal, why didn't you get here right away?" "Well," he explained, "I had a job to do." When I heard that story I better understood Ripken Junior's dedication. Like his dad, he does his job and then takes care of what ails him.

Nothing is as important to ballplayers as the respect of their peers. No one has more respect from his peers than Cal Ripken, Jr. Even without the record, he has been a two-time MVP, a perennial All-Star, a former Gold Glover who made only three errors at short one season, and a sure first-ballot Hall of Famer. All that is to be respected, as are the three thousand career hits he will achieve in 1999. But it is the Streak that truly makes him special in every player's eyes. Other players are well aware that he has achieved an enviable record that no one will ever break and that resulted in appreciation from fans the likes of which only Lou Gehrig knew. (I don't mind being challenged on my assertion that Ripken's record will never be broken. Because if it ever happens, I will be dead.)

You could see the respect, admiration, and awe (and maybe envy) on the faces of the California Angels players on the night Gehrig's "unbreakable" record fell, during those glorious moments when Ripken circled the field and accepted the love of the fans. And you could see it on the faces of the New York Yankees last September 20. It was Joe Girardi's idea to give Ripken a team tribute. After the first batter of the game, when it was a hard fact that Ripken was not starting, all the Yankees climbed to the top of their dugout and doffed their caps in the direction of Ripken in the opposite dugout. It was an appropriately subtle yet heartfelt sign of respect from a classy bunch of players who were setting records of their own yet were humble enough to let Ripken know how much they appreciated what he had done for baseball. It was much,

much better than a gold watch. Ripken was surprised and visibly moved by the Yankees' magnanimous gesture. And as he resumed the unfamiliar position of benchwarmer, he may have found himself reflecting for the first time on all the fruits of his sixteen years of continuous labor.

Roger Clemens

Late in the season, *Sports Illustrated* ran an interesting article about American League Cy Young contenders. It included a revealing anecdote about Roger Clemens, the eventual winner. Apparently, when Clemens, who had lost his last start on May 29, was in the Toronto Blue Jays bullpen preparing for his next start on June 3, he gazed up at the scoreboard and was shocked to see a less than stellar 5-6 record by his name. He turned to his pitching coach, Mel Queen, and expressed embarrassment. His exact words were "That's not me."

The article went on to explain how what Clemens said in the bullpen that day was based in truth. The Clemens who had a 3.50 ERA bore only a passing resemblance to the dominant pitcher who'd gone 21-7 with a 2.06 ERA in his first year with the Blue Jays. Since early April, Clemens's patented leg drive, the essential ingredient in his power-pitching style, had been hampered by a slow-healing groin-muscle injury. More secret were his personal problems. The public rarely is aware of the difficulties players have with family and health issues, and that was the case with Clemens. Perhaps fans had read in the back of the sports pages how Clemens's beloved grandmother Myrtle Lee had died during spring training. But probably the *SI* article was what first made them aware of his mother's ongoing battle with emphysema back in Texas, and his wife Deb's brief hospitalization during the season. So Clemens found himself shuttling back and forth between Texas and wherever Toronto was playing. He tried to live up to his personal credo: No matter what problems a pitcher has in his personal life he must concentrate solely on baseball on the fifth day. But Clemens admitted that his manager, Tim Johnson, and Mel Queen both recognized "a slight difference in my intensity level."

Was Clemens able to turn it on when he set his mind to do it? Does Mark McGwire have muscles? Beginning June 3 against the Tigers to September 21 against the Orioles, Clemens won his next fifteen decisions, the longest winning streak in the majors since Gaylord Perry had fifteen straight victories for Cleveland in 1974. Whereas in his previous eleven starts, Roger had no complete games and no double-digit strikeout performances, in his twenty-two starts following his statement to Mel Queen he threw five low-hit complete games and had at least ten strikeouts eleven times. He really started sizzling in mid-August, striking out fifteen batters against Anaheim in eight-plus innings, and following that with three shutouts in a row, including an eighteen-strikeout performance against Kansas City—his highest total other than his two twenty-strikeout games. When he copped his twentieth win against six losses against the O's, he again fanned fifteen batters, the tenth time in his career he had at least fifteen. By the time the dust had settled, the once-struggling pitcher with a losing record had become the first pitcher since Sandy Koufax to win pitching's Triple Crown (with 20 wins, a 2.65 ERA, and 271 K's) two years in succession. In the Cy Young Award race, he was like a horse who struggled getting out of the gate but then took off down the stretch, sweeping past the front-runners one at a time—David Cone, Pedro Martinez, David Wells (for whom Clemens would be traded on February 18, 1999). After the season ended, he would be a unanimous choice in winning the award for an unprecedented fifth time.

Perhaps Clemens and Sammy Sosa were sprinkled by the same magical dust because, eerily, they went into superhuman overdrive at exactly the same time. After May 29, during the same time Clemens went 15-0, Sammy smashed an amazing fifty homers! To say that Clemens was in a zone is an understatement. He not only knew for a fact that he was unbeatable but also that he could get individual batters out with any pitch he threw. Employing a four-seam fastball in the high nineties, a two-seamer that runs in to right-handed batters, a hard slider, and a wicked splitter, Clemens typically would quickly get two strikes on hitters by making them foul off pitches, and then get strike three on either called strikes or swinging strikes, often on checked swings. (A strikeout pitcher like Greg Maddux rarely gets swinging strikeouts because he hasn't the velocity or splitter of Clemens.) Clemens has always had the riding fastball to blow away batters and the control to hit both corners with uncanny accuracy for called strikes. When he throws a fastball or slider just off the outside corner or the splitter just below the strike zone, he enjoys seeing batters futilely try to check their swings.

Not that Clemens will show any emotion on the mound. He has the inner fire that is present in all great competitors, yet comes across as being completely impassive, like Greg Maddux rather than Randy Johnson. When a batter looks at him, he sees someone who is as unfriendly as his reputation, who doesn't care about him as a batter or as a person. This is an ideal approach for a pitcher. In fact, Clemens's disdainful gaze is meant to make the batter feel like rubble, like nothing. He's as mean on the mound as Frank Robinson used to be at the plate. The Rocket Man has the keen competitive intellect to comprehend that his nasty demeanor gives him an edge over batters. It gets into their heads. And a slight mental edge over the batter is all a pitcher needs for success. (Juan Marichal would unnerve batters by rushing to the mound each inning, showing them he couldn't wait to get them out.) A pitcher can't be friendly to the opposition.

I remember how Pete Rose would go over to young opposing pitchers and try to endear himself to them. The flattered pitcher would think, "Wow, Pete Rose talked to me. What a nice thing to do." But Rose was not being nice. He was trying to take that competitive edge away from the pitcher, to pacify him. No batter even thinks of fraternizing with Clemens because he knows he'll get a first-pitch fastball under his chin. That's the way it should be. (Last year, when reliever Mel Rojas was having a horrible time with the Mets, he was the friendliest guy imaginable. When Hispanic opposition players would arrive at Shea it would be like old-home week; then Rojas would pitch to the opposition and get battered.)

In Clemens's case, it has taken more than a strong arm, competitive drive, and imposing glare to have kept him at the top of his profession for so many years. I think the key to his success each year and over his entire career has been his work ethic. When Clemens first came to the majors as the nineteenth pick of the draft, he actually had to convince the Boston Red Sox to let him run and work out as much as he was used to doing. I remember talking to Red Sox veteran right fielder Dwight Evans about Clemens in either 1986, when Clemens went 24-4, or in his twenty-win '87 season, and though outfielders almost never pay attention to what pitchers do to get in shape, Evans raved about the young sensation. "You can't believe how intelligently this guy works," he told me. "He doesn't only work hard, he works smart. He works on the right things to make him an effective pitcher." In other words, when Clemens works, particularly to build up his lower body, it is with his performance in mind, and you'd be surprised how few ballplayers, especially pitchers, are smart enough to do this. I think what stands out about Clemens, and makes him the ideal model for many young pitchers who have early success, is that he never has taken anything for granted. He has never rested on his laurels. Instead, he has worked relentlessly off the field in order to maintain his level of success on it. There is no doubt in my mind that when he received his fifth Cy Young Award, he immediately started thinking how hard he would have to work in order to win for the sixth time. (He would be trying to do this, it turned out, for the Yankees in 1999.) Clemens may say that his goal each season is to be one of the top three pitchers in the league, but he is only fully satisfied when he proves to be the best. That scary guy on the mound wants to be king of the mountain for as long as possible.

Jeff Kent

A year after becoming the first Giants second baseman to drive in over 120 runs since Rogers Hornsby in 1925, Jeff Kent became the first major-league second baseman since Hornsby in 1921 and 1922 to go over 120 RBIs in consecutive years. He matched the Rajah on September 21, when he followed an intentional walk to Barry Bonds with a key three-run homer off Jose Silva in an 8–1 victory over Pittsburgh that pulled the streaking Giants to within 3½ games in the NL wild-card race. It was Kent's career-high thirtieth homer, one more than his 1997 total. The next time up, he would be plunked by a pitch, proof that this cleanup hitter, who prior to 1997 had never had more than twenty-one homers and eighty RBIs in a season, had achieved slugger status.

Steadily productive down the stretch as the Giants managed to force a play-off for the wild-card spot in the postseason, Kent finished the season with 31 homers and 128 RBIs. And he put up those lofty numbers despite missing twenty-five games due to injury. Obviously Kent had developed into a reliable clutch hitter who delivered more often than not with men on base, as he proved himself capable of being in 1997, when he drove in 121 runs despite only a .250 average. I look at his numbers and can't help but be impressed. And surprised. Those were the types of power stats for a second baseman that we might have expected from Carlos Baerga in those years he was on a Hall of Fame track with Cleveland—not from a player who was no better than a fair hitter with moderate power during several unexciting years with the New York Mets. But Baerga's career went south, and Kent was the one who started hitting the longball. Some things in baseball are inexplicable, and Jeff Kent driving in 249 runs in two seasons is at the top of my list. Kent equaling Hornsby? It's as if Fabian were suddenly singing duets with Celine Dion and holding his own.

While a high RBI total is often a result of who is hitting in front of you—and I think many of the runs Kent drove in were because of them—you still have to give him credit for producing. I also credit Dusty Baker. Significantly, he put Kent in the four-spot to protect Bonds although Kent showed no indication in the past that he would be a potent cleanup hitter. Also Baker, the rare manager who really knows what makes people tick, turned an often dour player into someone who received votes in the National League's Most Valuable Player balloting. Baker will tolerate his being a defensive liability at second base, because nowadays at the plate Jeff Kent becomes Clark Kent.

Jason Kendall

It's not often that the record book must be altered in back-to-back innings, but it happened during the Giants' 8–1 victory over the host Pittsburgh Pirates on September 21. In the sixth inning, one inning after the Giants' Jeff Kent became the second second baseman to drive in over 120 runs in successive innings, the Pirates' Jason Kendall became the first catcher in National League history to steal twenty-six bases in a season. Kendall broke the record that was set by the Mets' John Stearns in 1978. Before scoring the Bucs' only run of the game, the excited Kendall asked that he be given the base as a souvenir of his big moment. "It's something I can remember forever," he mused later in the locker room. "It's not quite Barry Bonds's forty-forty, but to me it's real special."

When Kendall was a rookie, Jim Leyland, who was then Pittsburgh's manager, told me, "He probably shouldn't be up with us now because he might not be ready. But this kid is going to be a hell of a player." I didn't know much about Kendall at the time other than that his father was the former major league catcher Fred Kendall, whom I'd played against when he was on the Padres. However, I knew that when Leyland made a point of saying something about a player it merited attention, because he hasn't been wrong too often. So from that day forward I watched the young catcher's progress closely. As it turned out, Leyland was mistaken only about Kendall's readiness for the big leagues. The twenty-two-year-old became the fifth rookie catcher to be named to an All-Star team, batted a cool .300, made steady progress as a defensive catcher, and finished third in the voting for NL Rookie of the Year. But Leyland was on target with his prediction about Kendall's future. The early breakthrough year for Kendall came in 1998, when he improved dramatically in almost every statistical category. In 1997, he had eight homers, forty-nine RBIs, and a .294 average, and everyone in the Pirates organization was delighted. In July of a 1998 season in which he'd finish with twelve homers, seventy-five RBIs, a .327 average, and eight more steals, the organization was so dazzled that they signed the twenty-four-year-old to a four-year contract extension.

Kendall hasn't gotten much notice from fans around the country because he has played with a noncontender. Even in Pittsburgh he hasn't attracted proper attention because the Pirates have continued to draw only meager crowds unless Mark McGwire comes to town. In fact, less than sixteen thousand fans were present the day Kendall made second base his own. But at least his record got him more national attention than when he was a rookie and set the more dubious NL record for catchers of being hit by a pitch fifteen times in one year. He deserves the spotlight because he is one of baseball's rising young stars. After only three years in the league, he does everything well. He's an excellent hitter who has been slotted in the coveted third spot in the Pirates' lineup. As a catcher, he throws well, does a good job blocking balls in the dirt, calls a good game, and is very conscientious about all his responsibilities. And he's an excellent base runner with above-average speed. It's not just that he steals bases, but that he takes the extra base rather than playing it conservatively. I'm impressed that he takes pride in his base running. Because he possesses the skills and toughness that remind people of Craig Biggio, it was thought for a time that Kendall also would be converted into a second baseman. But that idea has been scrapped. The Pirates are more than content to have a young All-Star caliber catcher who will only get better. He could easily break John Wathan's major league record of thirty-six steals by a receiver, but I think the many other things he will accomplish will be far more exciting. Rarely in baseball history has a catcher been referred to as a great all-around player, but at a young age Jason Kendall is almost there.

Craig Biggio

One of the reasons baseball was so exciting last year is that so many records that were broken or equaled in 1998 were set in bygone eras. Craig Biggio, himself a throwback to those super-aggressive, caution-to-the-wind players of the distant past, was able to match a record that was set eighty-six years before! With a steal of second base in a 7–1 road victory over St. Louis, the Astros' lead-off man became the only modern-era player other than baseball immortal Tris Speaker to have fifty steals and fifty doubles in the same season. Considering that in addition to hitting those two-baggers and swiping second at an equal clip, Biggio played second base, it is likely that he also set the all-time records for both being around and touching second base in a season.

If Biggio were still a catcher he'd have broken the seasonal stolen-base record for that position four times already. But he was moved to second in 1992, the year after he became the first Astros catcher named to the National League's All-Star team. In 1992, he was selected as a second baseman, thus becoming the first player in major league history to have made the elite roster as both a receiver and a second sacker. In 1995, he became the first Astros player since 1973 to be chosen by the fans to start the Summer Classic. Since then he has settled in as the NL starting second baseman. In fact, many people who watch Biggio turn the double play as well as any second baseman in the league forget that he was a receiver in his first four years with the Astros and when he starred for Seton Hall University.

The Astros decided to move Biggio from the catching position because he had the strong arm, speed, and range (not to mention a catcher's love of contact) that would make him an ideal artificial-turf second baseman. He had the requirements, but Craig had to make himself into a superb fielder. For instance, he spent countless hours with Astros coach Matt Galante working on his footwork, applying those quick, short steps he'd done for years behind the plate to his pivot move. I know about that work because Yogi Berra told me, and Yogi always knows what he's talking about. Berra has had strong ties with the Astros since he ended his coaching career there, and the players he has kept in closest contact with have been Jeff Bagwell and Craig Biggio, the two guys who have meant the most to the organization. In fact, he always checks up on them when Houston comes into New York to play the Mets, and if things are going bad, he'll offer his wise counsel. Yogi, who is a great communicator, has told me that he likes Jeff and Craig because despite all their success, they pay attention, they listen. I think Yogi, a three-time MVP who knows the hard work that it takes to be a valuable, winning ballplayer, pretty much serves as their conscience. Today, there aren't too many more valuable, winning ballplayers than Bagwell, who was the NL's MVP in 1994, and Biggio, who could have won a couple of awards in the last four years but fell short in the balloting.

Both Biggio and Bagwell play the game with such intensity and dedication, yet it may seem strange to link the leadoff man to the cleanup hitter. After all, Craig's body isn't particularly strong and Jeff is built like an armored truck. Craig looks neither fast nor durable, somebody you'd pick last if you were choosing up sides. But his body can do all the things it tells us that it can't do, almost all the things Bagwell's does and a few it doesn't. It can play over 160 games; withstand the wear and tear of playing second base; smack fifty doubles and smash twenty homers; average about 125 runs a season (including 146 in '97); be hit by pitches at a league-leading clip; steal fifty bases; take out fielders with hard slides; and get down the first-base line so quickly that in 1997 he became the first player—remember, he's a right-handed hitter—not to ground into a double play in a 162-game season. A Gold Glover, a run-scoring machine, he is always in the thick of the action. Watch him in the dugout during a close game and you'll see a caged animal; you know he's wishing the rules could be changed so he could bat three or four times every inning, or pinch-run for all of his teammates. When you talk about guys who put their bodies on the line, you start with Biggio. When the dust clears, he's the guy who gets up from the bottom of the pile. His uniform is dirty when he puts it on before the game. When it's clean it's dirty because nobody can get the stains out anymore. And why bother?

Usually when you talk up a guy who plays like Biggio, you look at his so-so stats and quickly hedge, "But don't look up his numbers because they don't show all the intangibles that add to his worth." But Biggio has proved to be an Eddie Stanky type with intangibles *and* great statistics. Most impressively, most of his key numbers last year—210 hits, 51 doubles, 50 stolen bases, a .503 slugging percentage, and .325 average—were career highs. The numbers show that Biggio is improving! In that case, a year in the near future in which Biggio clubs 60 doubles and steals 60 bases is not out of the question. Not even Tris Speaker did that.

Tom Gordon

The Boston Red Sox may have finished light-years behind the New York Yankees in the American League East,
but they won the second most games in the league, thanks
in great part to two one-two punches: outstanding hitters
Mo Vaughn and Nomar Garciaparra; and outstanding
pitchers Pedro Martinez and closer Tom Gordon. Of the
four, only Gordon far exceeded preseason expectations.
Although he'd surprised everyone during the last six
weeks of 1997 after manager Jimy Williams shrewdly
switched him from the rotation into the stopper role, his
eleven saves gave him only fourteen for his entire career.
When Dennis Eckersley was signed as a free agent, it was
to give the Red Sox a fall-back guy if Gordon couldn't handle the job. But the thirty-year-old right-hander surprised

everyone by leading the American League with forty-six saves and setting a Sox record by finishing sixty-nine of the seventy-three games in which he appeared, surpassing "The Monster," Dick Radatz, who had sixty-seven finishes back in 1964.

Gordon's biggest save came, fittingly, on the Red Sox' biggest night of the year, September 24. The 30,997 anxious fans at Fenway Park were on their feet numerous times as the Red Sox won their ninetieth game for the first time since 1986 and nailed down a wild-card berth in the play-offs with a 9–6 victory over the Baltimore Orioles. They gave Vaughn an ovation when he got his two hundredth hit of the season and twice jumped to their feet as Garciaparra circled the bases, having belted his thirty-fourth and thirty-fifth homers of the year. And though starter Martinez had a shaky outing, he received respectful applause when he was relieved by Greg Swindell in the seventh inning because he left the game with a lead and the opportunity to win his nineteenth game of the season. There was another ovation in the eighth inning, when Dennis Eckersley made his 1,070th pitching appearance, tying Hoyt Wilhelm's major league record. Once the game's greatest reliever, Eckersley knew he'd turn the Sox' 9–6 lead over to Gordon to begin the ninth inning. He'd been doing it all year. When Gordon recorded his last save it had been his forty-first consecutive conversion (all since losing to the A's on April 10), and it broke the American League record that, ironically, Eckersley had set with Oakland in 1991 and 1992. On this night, Gordon would go for the major league record of forty-two straight saves, one more than the mark he held jointly with Trevor Hoffman and Rod Beck.

The crowd rose as one when Gordon came into the game, and they never sat down again. Unlike Rod Beck, Gordon would not get himself into a jam and then try to wiggle out of it. He knew the Fenway faithful were waiting for the final out before pandemonium would break loose. And that his Red Sox teammates wanted to rush into the clubhouse and revel in champagne, cigars, and, best of all, T-shirts with "Wild Card" emblazoned on them. On fifteen pitches, Gordon struck out Rich Becker, Mike Bordick, and Roberto Alomar in succession to claim the save record for himself, clinch Martinez's nineteenth victory, and give his team its first play-off berth since 1995. And the fans went wild.

Gordon's emergence as the league's top reliever was one of the great stories of the year. You may remember that Gordon was one of baseball's most touted young pitchers after he went 17-9 (10-2 as a setup man) for the Kansas City Royals in his 1989 rookie season. He threw so hard that Tom soon was replaced by "Flash," and everyone expected that he was only a year or two from becoming one of the game's most dominant pitchers. However, it wasn't to be. While he wouldn't turn out to be a "Flash" in the pan, this five-foot-nine flamethrower became for a time the definition of an average pitcher: He never topped the twelve victories he achieved in four different seasons and compiled a 78-79 record as a starter and long reliever in subsequent years with the Royals and, beginning in 1996, Red Sox. But in truth, as a full-time starter with the Royals and Red Sox, he got worse. Everybody could see it: Gordon was being pounded.

When Sox manager Jimy Williams and his pitching coach Joe Kerrigan decided to convert Gordon into a closer during the last six weeks of the 1997 season, their starter had been doing so poorly that they probably figured they had nothing to lose. However, the usual determining factor in deciding if a pitcher should be made into a short reliever is how he does if he pitches one time through a lineup. Gordon has a super fastball and a wicked twelve-to-six curve that rivals Darryl Kile's as the best in the game, but only Sandy Koufax could go through a lineup three or four times with just two pitches. By the second and third time batters saw Gordon in a game, they knew what to expect, and when major league ballplayers know what's coming they show no mercy. However, what would happen if a failed starter like Gordon were expected to face not nineteen or twenty-seven or more batters, but five or six at the most? As it turned out, Gordon was a failed starter who could mow down batters who would see him only once in a game. In fact, because he no longer had to pace himself for a long pitching stint, the speed on his fastball increased dramatically, back to about 96 mph.

I would guess that it wasn't that Gordon throws only two quality pitches that kept anyone from turning him into a stopper earlier, but that one of those pitches is a curveball. It makes sense that John Wetteland is probably the only other quality reliever who employs the curve with regularity. Significantly, relievers want to throw pitches that induce grounders, and the curve is not necessarily a groundball pitch—a batter may hit the curve on the ground, but the pitch is not designed to cause him to do that. More worrisome, perhaps, is that to throw his best curve, a pitcher, generally speaking, must go into his full windup, and that is not a luxury relievers have when they enter with men on base. Gordon has succeeded largely because he knows the correct times when he should throw his fastball and when he can go to the curve. When he does throw his breaking ball, he doesn't lose much speed. "What amazes me," Dennis Eckersley raved late in the season, "is the consistency of his velocity. I [see every day just] how nasty his curveball is." If Dennis Eckersley, who is Hall of Fame bound because of his own stopper credentials, marveled at Gordon last year, then you know just how awesome he was. According to Boston sportswriter George Kimball, my beautifully weird pal Bill Lee, who did a fair amount of fancy pitching in Fenway some years back, once hypothesized that the ultimate reliever will be someone who, through brain waves or something (who could really understand the Spaceman?), could seemingly make the ball disappear, only to materialize again in the catcher's mitt for a strike. Last year, probably many batters who faced Gordon, including the three Orioles who struck out when he secured his record-setting save, believed that was exactly what happened with some of Gordon's pitches. At those moments Flash Gordon was Bill Lee's ultimate reliever.

The New York Yankees

Interestingly, Joe Torre managed the Yankees' 160th game of the season on September 25 as if it were a tuneup for the postseason and not as if it were a game of historic significance. With a victory over the expansion Tampa Bay Devil Rays before 32,447 proud fans at Yankee Stadium, the Bronx Bombers—another amazing story of 1998—would win their 112th game of the season and pass the 1954 Cleveland Indians for the most wins by an American League club. But that didn't seem to affect Torre's decision on how best to utilize his players. After starter Orlando Hernandez had pitched the five innings necessary to record his twelfth victory, Torre let struggling starter Andy Pettitte get in three innings of work, and then brought in closer Mariano Rivera for one inning of needed fine-tuning in a nonsave situation. Also, by the end of the game, four players in the starting lineup were on the bench resting. It's true that the Yankees led 6–1 (the final score) after three innings against the last-place Devil Rays, but Torre might have made these changes even if the score were closer. I think he wanted to impress upon his players that the postseason now took precedence over the Yankees' setting a record—but I think he knew this Yankee team would win this game no matter who was out there. They weren't going to blow a five-run lead, especially with the record on the line. With the record in sight for a week, his team had gone on a roll rather than succumbed to pressure. And with this victory over Tampa Bay, a day after passing the legendary 1927 Yankees for the most wins in franchise history, New York won its fifth straight game and passed the '54 Indians. They would close the season by beating the Devil Rays twice more to establish the AL record of 114 victories, just two behind the major league mark set by the 1906 Chicago Cubs. The Yankees would have such a successful postseason, going 11-2, that almost everybody forgets that they ended their magical regular season with seven consecutive victories.

You will hear people say that certain championship teams "win the games they have to win," but as their final two victories signified, the '98 Yankees also made sure to win the games they didn't have to win. A team that took the lead in a modern-era-record forty-eight straight games in July and August, these Yankees had a gluttonous appetite for victories. How often we saw the ebullient smiles of Yankee players—Bernie Williams, David Wells, Scott Brosius, Mariano Rivera, Derek Jeter, Darryl Strawberry, to name a few—following big victories. You can't fake that. The Yankees loved to win so much that they were the first team of the modern era to have a winning percentage of over .700 for each of four straight months; and the second team ever to go twenty-four consecutive series before losing one. It was as if they wanted to prove George Steinbrenner had almost been prescient when he jokingly predicted a 162-0 record after looking at the '98 roster. (A 1-3 start on the West Coast ended such thoughts and had the New York press temporarily talking about Steinbrenner firing Torre. But Torre remained calm. The only time he lashed out at the team for lackadaisical play was in mid-September, during a series with Tampa Bay.)

This Yankee team not only wanted to win, but knew just how to do it and, as you understood when you surveyed their confident faces in the dugout, expected to rally for victory even when trailing. It was almost as if they'd gazed into a crystal ball and knew exactly how many runs their opponents would score each game, because they seemed to know whether they could rely on good pitching for a victory or needed to bring out the big bats. Methodically, they won both low-scoring games and high-scoring games, won by shutouts or blowouts when needed. On a given day, they could out-slug you, out-pitch you, out-field you, out-run you; they could do anything that was required to win the game. Among their most memorable victories:

- On April 4, in the Yankees' seventy-fifth home opener, they won a seesaw affair with the Oakland A's 17–13, the highest-scoring game in Yankee Stadium history.

- On May 17, they beat the Twins 4–0 as David Wells threw the first regular-season perfect game in Yankee Stadium history.

- On May 19, they came from behind on a three-run homer by Bernie Williams to defeat the Baltimore Orioles 9–5 and also won a brawl that began when frustrated O's reliever Armando Benitez hit Tino Martinez in the back after yielding Williams's blast. The humiliating defeat was the beginning of the end for the O's, who had been regarded as the Yankees' major challenger.

- On June 3, they beat visiting Tampa Bay 6–0 as Orlando Hernandez made his major league debut (after David Cone was bitten by his mother's terrier) and pitched seven strong innings.

- On June 15, they scored on a bases-loaded hit batsman and nipped the visiting Orioles 1–0 behind Cone. Their 61-20 record at the All-Star break was the best in the majors in the twentieth century.

- On August 4, they swept a twin bill from the A's in Oakland by winning the nightcap 10–5 with a nine-run ninth inning, highlighted by Darryl Strawberry's AL-record-setting second pinch-hit grand slam of the season.

- On August 16, on the fiftieth anniversary of Babe Ruth's death, they beat the Rangers 6–5 on a ninth-inning Ruthian blast into the upper deck at Yankee Stadium by Bernie Williams. In their 120th game, the Yankees joined the 1944 Cardinals as the fastest teams to reach ninety victories in a season.

- On August 18, they edged Kansas City 3–2 on a thirteenth-inning single by Chad Curtis. They won the season series with the Royals 10–0 to complete their first sweep of another team in their ninety-six-year history.

- On August 29, they defeated the Mariners in Seattle 11–6 behind Derek Jeter's seventeenth home run, a record for a Yankee shortstop, to up their record to 98-36 and clinch a postseason spot the earliest in team history.

- On September 4, they beat the White Sox 11–6 behind two Bernie Williams homers to go to 100-38, winning 100 games faster than any team in AL history.

- On September 20, they defeated the Orioles 5–4 in Baltimore when Cal Ripken, Jr., sat out for the first time since 1982.

- On September 23, they beat the visiting Indians 8–4 to tie the 1927 Yankees with 110 victories. Coal-hot rookie Shane Spencer hit his seventh homer.

- On September 24, they beat Tampa Bay 5–2 to tie the 1954 Indians with 111 victories. Spencer's eighth homer and second grand slam was the difference.

- On September 25, they won their 112th game against Tampa Bay, 6–1, to set an American League record.

- On September 26, they extended their record to 113 wins, 3–1 over Tampa Bay, as Mariano Rivera barely managed to save David Cone's twentieth victory. This was the first time Cone had won twenty games since he was 20-3 in 1988, longer by two years than Jim Kaat's record for years between twenty-win seasons. Spencer hit his ninth homer.

• On September 27, they finished the regular season with their AL-record 114th victory, 8–3, as Williams copped the batting title and Spencer clubbed his tenth homer, a record-tying third grand slam of the month.

It wasn't just the staggering victory total but the way the Yankees dominated opponents that caused many baseball pundits to suggest that they might be the best team of all time. I think comparisons to the '06 Cubs, '27 Yankees, '32 Yanks, Yanks of 1949–53, '54 Indians, '57 Braves, '61 Yankees, '70 Orioles, A's of the seventies, the 1976 Big Red Machine, and any of baseball's most heralded teams are entirely justified. It has been pointed out that this Yankee team, unlike those other teams, didn't have any sure Hall of Famers—though the jury is out on Derek Jeter, in only his third season—but they have had one or more Hall of Fame–caliber seasons. Last year, Jeter (3rd), Bernie Williams (7th), Paul O'Neill (12th), and David Wells (16th) were among the leaders in the MVP race. Perhaps few of the '98 Yankees will be listed as the greatest at their positions when this era is examined years from now, but for now, while they are in their primes, several of the position players (and several pitchers) deserve to be classified as great. The everyday lineup reads like an All-Star team, with future and past All-Stars waiting on the bench for spot starts. "People say they don't have superstars," said Paul Molitor during the World Series, "but they have a handful of guys who, if you put them on another club, would be superstars." As individuals, the Yankees didn't have overwhelming statistics, yet four regulars batted over .300 (Williams, Jeter, Paul O'Neill, and the surprising Scott Brosius); five scored 91 runs or more (Jeter, Chuck Knoblauch, Williams, O'Neill, and Tino Martinez), and four drove in 97 runs or more (Martinez, O'Neill, Brosius, and Williams). Also, in limited playing time Shane Spencer (10 HR, 27 RBI, .373 BA in 67 at-bats) and Darryl Strawberry (24 HR, 57 RBI in 295 at-bats) were extremely productive. Significantly, when the individual stats are totaled up they become extraordinary team stats. For example, the Yankees tied the major-league record by having six players in double figures in home runs and stolen bases. Also, the Yankees, who had ten players with at least 10 homers, had 207 homers overall, the most ever by a team without a 30-homer hitter.

A toxic mix of smarts and talent, the Yankee hitters simply wore down opposing pitchers in 1998 by working long counts and then either drawing walks or pouncing when the pitcher was forced to throw a predictable pitch for a strike. As Jim Leyland pointed out to me, these batters were so dangerous because as soon as pitchers were onto the fact that they liked to go deep in the count and decided to throw first-pitch strikes to get ahead, they became a lineup of first-ball hitters. It was as if they were all of one mind at the plate. This was equally true when they were on the bases. Following Joe Torre's instructions, every player ran hard to first, challenged outfielders' suspect arms by taking the extra base, and stole when the opportunity presented itself. Paul O'Neill isn't blessed with great speed but he was successful on fifteen of sixteen attempts, and almost every time he succeeded he came around to score a key run.

O'Neill was again the team's most dangerous hitter because of his ability to take the ball the other way with two strikes and because he out-thinks pitchers. He's probably the only batter other than Tony Gwynn who can look for the curveball and adjust to the fastball. He's also the Yankees' best outfielder despite having only average speed. He invariably catches the ball in correct position to throw. In building team chemistry, Torre allows players to feed off one another, and O'Neill was to everyday players what David Cone was to the pitchers. O'Neill set the tone. Once I asked Joe why his team was playing like it was only two games ahead instead of fifteen games ahead in the AL East race and he explained, "Nobody on this team ever gives up an at-bat because they look at O'Neill and see what every at-bat means to him. So they never let up." I once said on the air that O'Neill treats every plate appearance as if it were Armageddon. An out by O'Neill can result in smashed batting helmets, cracked bats, dented water coolers, and a litany of self-deprecating words. Torre says that when he hears O'Neill screaming and cursing up the tunnel after he has made a meaningless out, it's fine with him as long as Paul doesn't hurt himself. That's because Joe wants all the other players to hear the tirade and be inspired. (Last year, after O'Neill had made his eighth straight out, he was sitting on the bench and letting everyone know that he was thinking of retiring and returning to Cincinnati. That's when Don Zimmer said, "I've got a good friend in construction in Cincy, just give me the word and I'll get you a job. Pays much more than your job now, right, Paul?" And O'Neill, who knows he's prone to go overboard, just broke up.)

Balance is the key to a team having success, and one statistic proves that the '98 Yankees had just that: They led the league both in runs scored and fewest runs allowed. The batters and pitchers fed off one another just like the offense and defense do on a well-rounded football team. As solid as were the Yankees' position players offensively in '98, it was the Yankees' outstanding pitching staff that necessitates their inclusion among baseball's greatest teams, and makes them better, in my opinion, than outstanding offensive-driven teams like the 1961 Yankees and 1976 Reds (both of which had better lineups). While the Yankee pitchers were excellent individually, they gave batters so many different looks that as a unit they were much better than that. These guys picked up one another, just like batters do.

David Wells and Andy Pettitte are both left-handers but are such different pitchers that Joe Torre can pitch them back-to-back against one team without worrying the opposing batters will easily adjust to the second guy. Wells will throw a high fastball and change, Pettitte a sinker and cut fastball in on the hands to right-handed batters. It is imperative that Pettitte get the ball down to be successful, but Wells throws the ball harder and can be effective up in the zone. Moreover, they are totally opposite mentally, in that Wells throws with abandon and Pettitte is so conscientious that it can be detrimental to him when things don't go well. If, for instance, Pettitte's sinker didn't dart in just like he wanted it to, he'll decide he has to work on it and work on it when all he really has to do is forget about the one bad sinker and throw another. Pettitte is such a perfectionist that, as Torre says, when he tries to fix something that isn't broken something else will break.

Right-hander David Cone, the leader of the staff and the person who has helped Wells fit in, continued his remarkable career in 1998 by being only one of three pitchers in the league with twenty victories. To show what kind of winner he is, in 1998 he lost two decisions in a row for the first time since 1995, a total of ninety-seven starts without successive losses that ranks second best in history. David still has a terrific fastball and a whole assortment of pitches, from curves to splitters. He's like the mound equivalent of golfer Phil Mickelson. Just as Mickelson invents trick shots, Cone invents pitches with which to throw batters off-stride. He'll vary his grips, put different pressures on the ball to get various actions, and throw from every arm angle. And he has the confidence to throw every pitch on any count to any hitter.

Cigar-smoking Cuban right-hander Orlando "El Duque" Hernandez, of indeterminate age, fled his country on something that floats and soon after was a starter in the Yankee rotation. I think he shocked everybody with his poise, gritty determination, and confidence. But as Joe Torre points out, after surviving on the high seas, pitching in New York would be easy. After earning eight dollars a month pitching in Cuba, how much pressure could there be pitching with a $6 million multiyear contract in his pocket? After Fidel, George is a piece of cake. On the mound, El Duque pretty much combines what all the other Yankee pitchers throw into one unique style. He's similar to Cone in that he isn't limited to the fastball when he falls behind in the count. I think he was encouraged by Cone's example to use different grips and any angles to turn one pitch, say a breaking ball, into two or three pitches. Most Latin American pitchers are not trained to use an over-the-top style, and Hernandez is all over the place with his delivery and release points, which completely baffles batters. Like Cone, he will use a sidearm delivery against left-handed batters. As a left-handed batter I would relish facing right-handed sidearmers because their pitches would come in on a level plane and be very easy to see. However, Hernandez uses a high leg kick to hide the ball. Whereas Juan Marichal had a high straight-leg lift, Hernandez has a bent knee. I've never seen anything like it. This is the only pitcher other than Bob Gibson who I think of as an athlete *first*. I love to watch Hernandez in the right-field corner working out before a game because he does all kinds of weird stretches, high kicks, and wind sprints, showing excellent speed. He could better showcase his versatility in the National League, where pitchers bat and run the bases.

Although culture shock has affected him much more than Hernandez, prized Japanese import Hideki Irabu showed much more poise in 1998 than he did in his brief and frustrating half-season with the Yankees in 1997. He spent time with pitching coach Mel Stottlemyre in an attempt to get his act together and it has paid off to a great extent. He exhibited none of the petulant behavior that characterized his bad performances in 1997. Overall, he had a decent season. Occasionally Irabu exhibited a dominating fastball and splitter working in tandem, but he still got into trouble when he fell behind in the count and couldn't use the splitter. I'm sure Irabu would prefer to be the top pitcher on the Yankee staff after being a superstar in Japan, but he's probably lucky to be holding off swingman Ramiro Mendoza for the number-five spot in a very strong rotation.

The Yankees backed their strong starters with terrific setup men, lefties Mike Stanton, who is good enough to be a closer, and cult hero Graeme Lloyd, and righties Jeff Nelson and Mendoza. Torre loves to righty-lefty other teams to death and then bring on his brilliant young closer Mariano Rivera in the ninth. Last year, there was a lot of skepticism about Rivera because his strikeout numbers went down drastically. But under Stottlemyre's tutelage, Rivera learned a cut fastball to induce grounders and this kept him from tiring at the end of the season, as he did in '97. Then in the '98 postseason, he was able to turn it up another notch. I love to watch Rivera because I'm always amazed by how hard he throws with such an easy delivery. The ball just explodes out of his hand. Batters who get only one chance against him in a game find him very deceptive. They look at the frail-looking pitcher on the mound and say, "How did he do that?"

As Joe Torre understands, great teams need good chemistry in order to fulfill their potential. Despite so many diverse personalities, the '98 Yankees got along as well with one another as any team in memory. They used to say of the old Boston Red Sox teams that when night came they needed twenty-five cabs for twenty-five players, but these Yankees went out together, hung out together, and, as players did in the old days, talked baseball. There were leaders like David Cone and Derek Jeter—whose culturally disparate teammates must have reminded him of his childhood pals; calming influences like catcher Joe Girardi ("I just trust him," says Torre, "I trust how he thinks and I trust his instincts on the field"); players who stirred the pot like David Wells; introspective guys like Bernie Williams; and veterans like Tim Raines, who kept everybody loose with his twenty-four handshakes for his twenty-four teammates. Plus a blend of young players and veterans who, taking their lead from their manager, all exuded remarkable class. "They have an inner conceit," said Torre. "They know they're good, but they don't have a need to flaunt it."

The '98 Yankees were definitely a great team. But the greatest? I'm sure the players realized that the 1906 Cubs and 1954 Indians lost their chances to claim that title by being upset in the World Series. The Yankees knew to a man that if the team was going to go down in history as being one of the best teams ever, even 114 victories would not be enough. They would have to win an unprecedented 125 games in 1998 to earn the respect they wanted. They would have to win the World Series.

Ken Griffey, Jr.

More than any other sport, baseball is dependent on its history, tradition, and nostalgia—memories both actual and perceived and statistics in record books and on the backs of bubblegum cards. The 1998 season certainly provided the vivid images and the astonishing numbers that will leave an indelible impression in the minds of all the fans who were fortunate enough to witness it. Still I think the remembrance of the season that we should most treasure is that so many of the greatest players of the entire era achieved something on the field that will be highlights of already spectacular careers. We saw exciting accomplishments by veterans at the ends of their careers and by brilliant newcomers such as Kerry Wood and Ben Grieve, yet what makes 1998 so momentous is that fans got to see amazing achievements by so many star players who are in their prime—the best from the best. It's startling how many great players in their peak baseball years came through with peak performances—nobody disappointed us—and rewrote the record book. This was definitely true of Mark McGwire and Sammy Sosa. And of Ken Griffey, Jr.

Time is so fleeting in baseball that entire careers flash past in the blink of an eye. Before we know it another dozen years will pass and Junior will be an old man by baseball standards, graying at the temples perhaps. It happened to Willie Mays. It happens to everyone. So that's why it's important that we store away memories of him while he is at his absolute best as a hitter, fielder, and base runner. Which he has been the past three seasons. Griffey plays the game so effortlessly that I'm sure many fans can't fully recognize the extent of his talent, or just how hard it is to accomplish what he does. There's a danger of our taking him for granted when we should be reveling in his performance. He's so much fun to watch because he's a guy who plays the game with such grace and such joy— he plays like a "Junior"—and is one of the few players who never talks about money once his contract is signed. A couple of years ago, I believed Barry Bonds was baseball's greatest player, but based on what Griffey has done in his 1997 MVP season and his equally magnificent but less publicized 1998 campaign, I would say that Griffey has ascended to the throne.

Although he is more intelligent about his image than Barry Bonds and acts playfully and flashes his magnetic

smile at times when Bonds may opt for off-putting arro-
gance, Griffey always has been aloof (perhaps protectively)
with the press and acted disinterested in discussing his
accomplishments as an individual in a team sport. This was
even more noticeable last season, when the Mariners were
out of contention and whatever the frustrated Griffey did
was not enough to reverse their descent into mediocrity.
However, while everybody was focused on the McGwire-
Sosa home-run chase, Griffey didn't merely show that he
could break records with the best of today's stars, but
confirmed his place among the greatest players of all time.
Junior quietly had an outstanding season in which he
reached a number of major milestones:

- On April 13, he belted two homers in a 6–5 loss to the
  Indians that gave him 300 for his career. At 28 years,
  143 days, he became the second-youngest player to
  reach that number, trailing only Jimmie Foxx's 27
  years, 328 days. (In 1997, he became the fourth-
  youngest player to hit 250 homers.)
- On June 30, he crushed his American League–leading
  33rd homer to pass his own 1994 league mark for most
  homers by the end of June.
- On July 14, he smashed his 38th and 39th homers in
  Seattle's 6–3 win over the Rangers, to give him his
  1,500th and 1,501st career hits. In his tenth major
  league season, he moved halfway to 3,000 hits.
- On September 7, the day on which McGwire moved
  three homers ahead of Sammy Sosa and tied Roger
  Maris's single-season record with his 61st homer, he

slammed his 49th and 50th homers in an 11–1 home victory over the Orioles. Having hit 56 in 1997, he joined Babe Ruth and McGwire as the only players to have consecutive seasons with 50 round-trippers. For the first time, three players (of an eventual four) reached the 50-homer mark in the same season.

- On September 15, he went deep for the 52nd time, had four hits and five RBIs in a 12–7 victory over the Twins. At 28 years and 10 months, he became the fourth-youngest player to drive in 1,000 runs in a career, trailing only Mel Ott, Jimmie Foxx, and Lou Gehrig.

- On September 16, he stole his 20th base in a 4–1 victory over the A's, and joined Willie Mays (1955) and Brady Anderson (1996) as the only major leaguers in history with 50 homers and 20 steals in a season.

- On September 22, in a 7–6 victory over the visiting A's, in which Alex Rodriguez set the AL record for homers by a shortstop with 41, he smashed his 54th and 55th homers to join Babe Ruth and Lou Gehrig as the only players to drive in 140 runs in three consecutive seasons. With the 54th homer, he and Ken Griffey, Sr., became the second father-son combination to hit 500 combined home runs, following Bobby and Barry Bonds. (This was the rare achievement that Griffey actually admitted was exciting to him.)

- On September 25, Griffey hit his 56th homer for the second consecutive year while driving in five runs in a 15–4 walloping of the Rangers. The fourth-inning blast off Eric Gunderson was his 21st homer of the year against left-handers, tying the major league mark set by Stan Musial in 1949 and equaled by Griffey in 1996. At 28 years and 308 days, he became the youngest player in history to belt 350 career homers.

Griffey expressed relief after he dropped out of the three-way race to surpass Roger Maris's seasonal home-run record, but with his final homer he moved into position to challenge Hank Aaron's career home-run record. I remember that when Aaron hit his 715th career homer to pass Babe Ruth and when he went on to record 755 homers before retiring, everybody said that there was no way anyone would ever even come close to him. We did the calculations and realized that if a batter had to average 40 homers a year for eighteen or nineteen years, the record was as safe as Cy Young's 511 career victories. But we weren't expecting a young player to come along and average 53 homers for a three-year period. He'll have to hit 40 homers for the next ten years to catch Aaron, but at this point no one thinks that is beyond his potential, as long as he stops running into walls in center field. Now if Griffey has a season in which he hits "only" 40 homers, we will want to know what's wrong with him. It's unfair maybe, but Griffey now makes us expect 50-homer seasons. Because he came to the big leagues at eighteen, Griffey would be only thirty-eight when he broke the record. That's why Aaron himself believes Junior will pass him. As a former player, I can tell you that 755 home runs is an incredible total. Frank Baker hit only 98 in his career— one more than me—and his nickname was "Home Run." Three hundred and fifty homers for a career has been accomplished by only fifty-two players in the history of the game.

Considering that Aaron and Griffey may end up one and two on the all-time homer list, it's interesting how different their batting styles are. Aaron would walk to the plate and stop and put his batting helmet on, and with the bat between his legs, he'd clear his throat with a slight cough and then step into the batter's box. I noticed that Aaron would never leave the box between pitches, even after foul balls. He had no unnecessary motions. He'd just relax at the plate, see the ball far better than mortal hitters, and keep his hands back so well that, unlike Griffey, he could hit off his front foot. Aaron, displaying the perfect swing and power, once hit a Curt Simmons curve I called for on top of the roof at Busch Stadium (only to be called out because his front foot was out of the batter's box), yet he wasn't someone you usually associated with loft. He hit a lot of line drives that just cleared fences about 335 feet away. He hit a lot of balls against the wall as well as over it. But when pitchers faced Aaron they knew there was a good chance he'd hit the ball hard when he made contact. However, Griffey's uppercut swing gives him tremendous loft and often results in long home runs, so the longball is at the forefront.

Griffey has a swing that starts and ends differently from any I've ever seen. It's an erect swing with a very high finish. Almost all other power hitters have their knees bent when they swing, just as boxers will rarely stand straight up when they throw a punch. But Griffey is upright and elegant, almost like the Colossus of Rhodes, and

gets extreme height in his follow-through. In case you wonder why other batters who want to hit homers don't use
that uppercut swing it's that without Griffey's super hand-
eye coordination, they would pop up everything. Anybody
with a loop in his swing is vulnerable to inside pitches, but
lesser batters than Griffey have much more trouble making contact. Pitchers do come inside to Griffey but it's to
get him out, not strike him out.

In his final years, Hank Aaron became so consumed by
his pursuit of Babe Ruth's record that he became identi-
fied almost exclusively with the home run in the eyes of
the fans. Because he could hit for average, drive in runs
even when he didn't homer, run (he was someone who
was never hurt and, unlike all the rest of us, *never* limped),
catch the ball, and throw, Aaron was a fantastic all-around
ballplayer, and would be talked about in the same way we
do Willie Mays if the home run hadn't become paramount.
I think that when Griffey repeatedly insists that he is not a
classic home-run hitter, he is trying to ensure that he will
be thought of like Mays. He'll probably be happier to break
Aaron's career RBI record than his home-run record because that will prove he is much more than a homer hitter.

I think Griffey isn't eager to participate in the annual
home-run contests prior to All-Star Games because he
doesn't want to be perceived as someone who deliberately goes for home runs. Considering that he was complaining about having messed up his regular swing during
the contest in 1997, it's clear that Griffey didn't devise his
patented swing to hit homers. I'm sure Griffey, who was on
his way to winning his second-consecutive AL homer title,

was happy to beat out Jim Thome in the contest in 1998, but there was probably some uneasiness to go along with the victory because it further connected him to home runs in the public's eye.

Interestingly, Griffey wasn't even going to participate until the Colorado fans, who felt it wouldn't be a real homer contest without him, booed him so hard during the daily workout that he felt compelled to throw his bat into the ring. It was a welcome turnaround. When he changed his mind, I saw that as confirmation that in 1998 players were making sure to be responsive to the fans. It was another instance where the fans saw that they were a big part of the game and even influenced the game. As in earlier decades, they felt there was a definite bond between them and their heroes.

Curt Schilling

The winds decreased from a brisk 20 mph to 10 mph during the course of a long Saturday afternoon, as the Phillies and host Marlins struggled through two extra-inning games. These were the final gasps of the deadly Hurricane Georges, which had caused postponements the previous two days and threatened to stick around long enough to prematurely end the baseball season for both teams. The thirty-six thousand fans, with slickers covering their smuggled-in chips and beer, appreciated being able to come to the park and watch baseball again. The last-place Marlins, embarrassed to have the worst record for any defending world champion in history, wanted to add victories to their meager total. And the Phillies' first-game starter, Curt Schilling, was grateful for a chance to pitch one more game and possibly add his name to the list of record-setters in 1998.

As the wind blew across the diamond in game one, Schilling blew away seven Marlins batters in eight innings in his final effort of the season. His last strikeout victim of the game, Kevin Orie, was his 300th of the year, which meant the Phillies right-hander could add his name to those of Rube Waddell, Sandy Koufax, Nolan Ryan, and J. R. Richard as the only pitchers in baseball history to have had consecutive 300-strikeout seasons. In 1997, Schilling fanned 317 batters in winning his first of back-to-back strikeout titles.

Pitchers don't like to say they try for strikeouts, but Schilling admitted afterward that he was going for the record against the Marlins. "I wanted it," he told reporters. "I'm proud I did it with everything that's going on here," he added, in reference to the destructive hurricane. "I was sure we were not going to play the series." By getting his final, record-tying strikeout in Florida, Schilling ended the season with 150 strikeouts at home and 150 strikeouts on the road, a sign of consistency that recalls Stan Musial getting 1,815 hits at home and exactly the same number on the road during a twenty-two-year career. Although the Phillies had a surprisingly good season in 1998, they were out of pennant contention early and weren't a drawing card, yet fans paid good bucks to see Schilling whenever he came to town. Partly it was to see one of the best pitchers in baseball; and partly it was to envision him in their team's starting rotation in the near future. That's because in the last few years, there have been extensive rumors that the rebuilding Phillies were talking trade with several teams about their high-priced ace. So fans wondered if Schilling was in fact "auditioning" for their front offices when he pitched in their ballparks. Who can forget the ovation the fans in Cleveland gave Schilling when he was introduced as part of the National League squad at the 1997 All-Star Game? At the time, a Schilling-to-Cleveland trade was almost a done deal, so the fans thought they were just welcoming him to their team. Of course, Schilling stuck with the Phillies and it was applause wasted.

It's easy to understand why general managers have been pestering the Phillies about Schilling's availability in the past few years. He'd be a tremendous addition to any team's pitching staff. First of all he has tremendous stuff. I think he's a bit like an NL version of Roger Clemens, which he'd take as a great compliment. He's a power pitcher with terrific control, the quintessential hard thrower who works fast and comes right at you. Some baseball people were referring to him as a "sinkerball pitcher" as late as 1997, but no sinkerballer throws 95 mph with regularity or strikes out over three hundred batters in a season. He may have thrown some two-strike two-seamers and splitters a while back, but he abandoned that when he realized batters couldn't get around on his high heater. That's his two-strike out pitch.

What I like best about Schilling is that he's a team player, which is true of few pitchers. He has taken it on himself as the veteran star of the Phillies (with gifted youngster Scott Rolen quickly on the rise) to be a leader in the clubhouse and a spokesman for the organization. He showed his loyalty to the franchise when he criticized top 1997 draft pick J. D. Drew (who eventually became a Cardinal) for insultingly turning down the huge contract he was offered by the Phillies' management. His loyalty to his teammates has been shown by how he has protected them. When a Phillies batter has been hit or knocked down, he has always retaliated with "message" pitches of his own. Quickly. Believe me, a six-foot-four, 230-pound pitcher with a heater and the control to throw the ball a short whisker under a chin can set things right in a hurry. I love his toughness. I remember a couple of years back when Deion Sanders was hotdogging off third and doing some other annoying things and Schilling told him, "You keep that stuff up and I'm going to drill you!" Sanders kept it up and Schilling was true to his word. And taking a page from Don Drysdale's book, he said to Sanders, "Here I am if you want me. I'm only sixty feet six inches away!" Deion didn't accept his challenge.

Being tough on the field doesn't imply he isn't a decent guy off it. I've always been moved by the Alaskan-born Schilling's attachment to his late father. He had died before Curt pitched in the 1993 World Series, yet Curt bought him a ticket to attend anyway. So when Curt was throwing a five-hit shutout in Game 5 against the Toronto Blue Jays, the camera focused on the seat in the stands that was reserved for his dad. Who knew a shot of an empty seat could be so emotional? Recently Curt told me that he still buys his father a seat to every game he pitches. I think baseball can do with such sentiment.

It remains to be seen whether the Phillies will build a team around Schilling or trade him for several prospects or everyday players. Certainly Schilling could get more money from another organization, but that has never struck me as his priority. I think he just wants to wear a major league uniform. Next year it will be fun watching Schilling as he tries to join Nolan Ryan as the only pitchers with three consecutive 300-strikeout seasons.

Rickey Henderson

Rickey Henderson has always turned it on when the cameras were on. No one in baseball more loves to put on a show, whether it's in the batter's box or on the basepaths or out in left, where the former Gold Glove winner tries to please those fans he gabs with during breaks in the game. Rickey has done whatever it takes to assure everyone that their eyes are on the right guy, no matter how many home-run hitters are on the field. That's why it was so predictable that he rose to the dramatic occasion when the Oakland Athletics honored him with "Rickey Henderson Day" on September 26. Sammy Sosa had his worst game of the year the day the Cubs gave him his day, but Rickey is much more comfortable with that type of attention. His average for the year would end up a dismal .236, but on his day he batted 1.000, going three-for-three, including a single in the ninth that beat the Anaheim Angels 4–3, and, most significant, he stole his sixty-fifth and sixty-sixth bases of the season. It was a day when he often flashed the most endearing and familiar smile in the game. Rickey—and he'll never be so old that we'll call him "Rick" Henderson—was again that young player who broke into the majors with the A's in 1979 and flew around the bases with childlike glee, the happy kid who was born on Christmas Day.

Sixty-six stolen bases, one for each Sammy Sosa homer, was twenty-one more than Henderson swiped in 1997 and his highest total since 1989, and it would be enough to lead the major leagues by a wide margin. In winning his first stolen-base title since 1991 and twelfth overall, the thirty-nine-year-old who was in his fourth stint with Oakland became the oldest player in history to lead his league in steals. Eddie Collins was thirty-seven when he established the record seventy-four years before! What Henderson did at thirty-nine may be as extraordinary as his stealing a record 130 bases in 1982 at the age of twenty-three.

Stealing that many bases at his age is much more impressive than forty-two-year-old Ted Williams hitting twenty-nine homers in his final season or Darrell Evans booming forty homers to lead the league at the age of thirty-eight: Players can maintain power much easier than speed. But Henderson is a unique specimen. A star running back in high school, he has thick, muscular thighs that almost burst through his pant legs and a chiseled upper body. One always thinks of Rickey as being playful and carefree, but I have seen how diligently he works on the weights. When his former Padres teammate Tony Gwynn, who works harder than anybody, says that he was inspired by Henderson's work ethic, that's an indication of Rickey's dedication to his game. He has always understood that for him to withstand the wear and tear of stealing bases and also accumulate 266 lifetime home runs (including a record for 73 lead-off homers), his entire body must have exceptional tone and strength.

I wasn't someone who criticized Henderson for "jaking it" when he missed a lot of games with the Yankees in the late 1980s because he claimed to have a hamstring pull that just wouldn't heal. I figured that he takes so much joy in playing the game that he wanted to be out on the field if he could. But I found it amusing that Rickey kept referring to his hurt "hammy" when he defended himself to the media. It was as if his "hammy" were tethered to his heart. Nobody had ever talked about a "hammy" before. Everybody in New York got tired of hearing about his hammy. In fact, some fan wrote to Mike Lupica at the New York *Daily News* and suggested that if Henderson were drafted by the expansion Marlins, they could dedicate the song "Moon over My Hammy" to him. Lupica wrote in his column, "I don't like his humor, but McCarver will." And I loved it.

Henderson ended the '98 season with 1,297 lifetime steals. It has been so long since he broke Lou Brock's major league record of 938 steals that we tend to forget that the record increases with each theft. The same thing happened when Nolan Ryan pulled away from Steve Carlton as the all-time strikeout leader. Then when Ryan retired, we saw that he was the all-time leader by 1,578 strikeouts, more than six years' worth of strikeouts! That Henderson, who signed a contract to play with the Mets in 1999, already has 359 more steals than anyone else in history is astounding. That may be the greatest of his many achievements.

I think what made Henderson into such a tremendous base stealer, besides his obvious running talent, is his admirable attitude that he isn't a base stealer at all but a run scorer. From the moment he steps to the plate he is thinking of circling the bases and returning to the plate, one run scored. That's why he immediately starts cajoling umpires into shrinking the strike zone so that he'll either receive a base on balls (he tied the A's record with 118 walks in 1998) or force the "squeezed" pitcher to throw a fat one. There's been nobody in the last twenty years who has made pitchers throw balls into a more predictable area than the game's best all-time leadoff hitter. Once on base, Henderson studies the pitcher's pickoff move and drives him to distraction as he edges from the base in that familiar crouch with his hands dangling low to the ground. Henderson and all expert base stealers realize that speed is not enough. A good jump is essential. He takes off with quick acceleration, running close to the ground. Increasingly he uses the dangerous hands-first slide, which young runners foolishly copy to be like their hero. Yes, he takes pride as he steals another base, but his real satisfaction comes from being one base closer to home.

Rickey wants to score runs. That has become his passion. In 1998, he became the oldest player since Sam Rice in 1930 to score one hundred runs in a season. It was the thirteenth time he passed the century mark. On August 31, when he homered, singled, and drew two walks against Cleveland, the future Hall of Famer scored his two thousandth run, joining Ty Cobb, Hank Aaron, Babe Ruth, Pete Rose, and Willie Mays as the only players to reach this milestone. Henderson has never said a word about how he will drive in one thousand runs from the leadoff position, but he will tell you that he wants to move up the ladder among the all-time scoring leaders. I don't know if he'll have enough time to reach his goal of passing Ty Cobb's record 2,246 runs in a career, but it will be great fun watching him add to his stolen-base records in order to do that. Because this geriatric wonder is still the best at what he does best. This may be the era of home-run hitters, but Rickey still wants our eyes on him.

Dennis Eckersley

At Fenway Park on September 26, 1960, Ted Williams crushed a Jack Fisher fastball into the right-center-field bullpen for his 521st homer in the final at-bat of a twenty-two-year career. It has become part of the Williams legend how he circled the bases—"like a feather caught in a vortex," wrote John Updike—disappeared into the dugout, and sat with his head against the wall, refusing to acknowledge the pleas from the fans, as well as the players and umpires, to make a curtain call. As Updike would explain, "Gods do not answer letters." Flash forward *exactly* thirty-eight years, to when Dennis Eckersley, making his final regular-season appearance in a twenty-four-year career, was visibly moved by the appreciative crowd's ovation as he sprinted in from the bullpen and took the mound. The knowledgeable Boston fans were cheering a long, eventful, and very strange career, including two stays in Boston, that guaranteed the league's oldest player would take his place alongside Williams in Cooperstown five years hence. On this night, Eckersley, forty-three, was putting a big exclamation point on that career, adding one more amazing accomplishment to his vita sheet. Maybe he wasn't going out in as dramatic a manner as Williams, but just by throwing his first pitch, Eckersley passed Hoyt Wilhelm for the most appearances in a career by a pitcher.

It's much more understandable how Wilhelm, whose twenty-one-year major league career concluded in 1972, could hold the record than Eckersley. After all, he threw a knuckler, an effortless technique pitch that will allow a pitcher, in theory, to pitch forever—and, in fact, Wilhelm didn't call it quits until he was forty-nine. Eckersley always threw hard stuff, a fastball and slider, and that takes its toll on arms and shoulders. Equally significant is that Wilhelm started only 51 games, so was able to pitch many games in relief year after year. On the other hand, Eckersley made 361 starts in the first part of his career—a career unto itself. In fact, one could think of his years as a starter with the Indians, Red Sox, and Cubs, from 1975 to 1986, as the "past life" of the reincarnated pitcher who was the quintessential reliever of the last dozen years. Highlights of that career included: throwing a shutout in his first start, as part of a record 28⅓ scoreless innings to begin a career; becoming only the eighth pitcher to strike out two hundred batters in a season before turning twenty-two; tossing a no-hitter in 1977; and winning twenty games for Boston in 1978.

Here was a guy in his early thirties who had won 151 games as a very good starter and would, when everyone could see he was finished and thought he should retire, become a reliever and go on to save 388 games (of his American League–record 390 saves). It's unfathomable. What makes Eckersley stand out in my mind is how he was able to go from good to awful to great; nobody else has been on the bottom rung of the ladder and leapt to the top, bypassing all the steps in between. And Eckersley really was at the bottom in his final days with the Chicago Cubs. Eager hitters just said, "Give me a bat! Let me at 'im!" To realize how low Eckersley had gone on the pitching totem pole, one only has to look at the names of the three players Chicago got in return for him (and Dan Rohn) from the Oakland A's early in the 1986 season: Dave Wilder, Brian Guinn, and Mark Leonette. Who? Talk about highway robbery.

While Eckersley credits AA and his wife's support for helping him win his battle with booze, credit for his on-field resurrection must go to then–A's manager Tony La Russa and his pitching coach, Dave Duncan. Having just converted Dave Stewart from a reliever to a starter who would win twenty games four straight seasons, they did the reverse with Eckersley, permanently moving him to the pen and, after Jay Howell's injury, into the closer role. They made this move although Eckersley had pitched in relief only one time, with the Cubs the previous year, ending a string of 301 consecutive starts dating back to 1976! Obviously, the born-again pitcher had found his calling. Beginning in 1987, when he led the league with forty-five saves, he had a record string of six consecutive thirty-save seasons for several outstanding A's teams, including a personal-best fifty-one in 1992. There's no sure thing in baseball, but the Eck came mighty close. At one point the A's won fifty-three straight games in which he appeared. It's a testament to his greatness that he could yield that storied game-winning home run to Kirk Gibson in the first game of the 1988 World Series and also a game-tying ninth-inning homer to Roberto Alomar in the 1991 ALCS play-offs and still hold his head high, content that he had achieved so much in pennant races, All-Star Games, and the postseason that he was entitled to an occasional failure. He just went back out on the mound and continued to excel, year after year. In 1992, he had a microscopic 0.61 ERA in 73⅓ innings, the lowest in major league history for a pitcher who threw at least 25 innings. And in the final year of his prime, 1992, he was both the Cy Young winner and the AL's MVP.

And he did it with style. He'd charge in from the bullpen like a gunfighter hired to bring order to the chaos in town. You could see him at the O.K. Corral—of course he was much better than O.K. He even had the look of a frontier hero, with the droopy mustache and long hair, and it was amazing how someone with such a charming smile could look so menacing when he *didn't* smile. And when he struck out a batter in game-deciding situations, with pitches that seemed to bear bat repellent, he'd pump his fist into the air and shout triumphantly, an action that often caused opposing teams to vow revenge. But he didn't care about that. He had an aura of invincibility, a belief that no one could hit him.

How Eckersley became a one-per-inning strikeout pitcher during his years with Oakland is perhaps the greatest mystery. I can look at Randy Johnson and say, "He can do that!" And the same goes for Roger Clemens and Kerry Wood. But I looked at Eckersley and said, "How can he do that?" Because he was a guy with a light fastball. He got away with it because he hid the ball behind a high leg kick, had that imposing look, was just so damn competitive, and, most significant, invariably got ahead in the count and put batters in a defensive mode. First pitch, first strike. And then he went to work. From 1988 to 1990, he struck out 198 batters in 203⅔ innings and walked a grand total of 16 batters! That's stupendous control. And when you consider that there were only 125 hits against him in those three years, you really become aware of how stingy he was with base runners.

I thought Eckersley should have retired before last season. He had a couple of thirty-save seasons with the Cardinals after leaving the A's, but even then it was obvious that his skills had diminished considerably. He could still get right-handed batters out with sliders away, but as his infamous sliders to Kirk Gibson and Roberto Alomar gave hint of, his sliders to left-handed batters began to flatten out with increasing frequency. Returning this year to Boston, near his home, he could no longer work as a closer so was relegated to being a setup man for Tom Gordon. I wondered why he didn't quit rather than make such a change, but I underestimated his competitiveness. And now that Eckersley has retired, I'm glad he was able to stick around and both achieve his final record and receive the final of many ovations the hometown fans gave him during the year.

And I was glad to see that when he did retire in December, he was fully reconciled to finally walk away from the game he loved. He understood that he had done the impossible, surviving battles and tremendous pressure on and off the diamond, and that now he could finally relax. "I had a good run," an emotional Eckersley said, "I had some magic that was with me for a long time, so I know that I was real lucky to not have my arm fall off—to make it this long physically is tough enough. [T]o me, it's like you're being rescued too when your career's over. It's like, 'Whew, the pressure's off.' "

Shane Spencer

The New York Yankees concluded their magical season on September 27 by extending their American League–record number of wins to 114 as they steamrolled the Tampa Bay Devil Rays, 8–3. It was "Joe DiMaggio Day" at Yankee Stadium, and appropriately Bernie Williams went two-for-two to finish the season at .339, two points ahead of Boston's Mo Vaughn, and joined the Yankee Clipper and Mickey Mantle as Yankee center fielders who have won batting titles. Yes, it was a big day for Williams, but like all the other established stars in the Yankee lineup who had been ripping the ball during the final month, he would find himself sharing the next day's headlines with September sensation Shane Spencer. The late-season call-up had only one hit in the game, but it was his third grand slam of the month! That equaled the same major league record that Mike Piazza tied with the Dodgers in April and tied him for the American League lead for the full season with Orioles catcher Chris Hoiles.

His manager, Joe Torre, was understandably amazed by Spencer's accomplishment because Torre managed to hit three grand slams in his entire career in 7,874 at-bats. Spencer had done it in only 67 at-bats! Moreover, he'd smashed two homers in late August and eight in September in 38 at-bats to set a Yankees rookie record for the month, driven in twenty-seven runs (twenty-one in September) and batted a gaudy .373 (.421 in September). And more often than not his homers and other hits came in clutch situations. It was quite a hot period for a twenty-six-year-old who had been languishing in the Yankee system for eight years, who was given a chance to play on a team that didn't seem to need anyone new. From out of nowhere he emerged as the Yankees' best hitter during the last month and certainly was a factor in their securing the record number of victories. Torre told me that he couldn't believe what he was seeing game after game. In fact, Spencer hit so well that he forced Joe to put him on the Yankees' postseason roster, even before Darryl Strawberry was diagnosed with colon cancer. Torre, whose streak of good luck continued with the emergence of Spencer, had to thank the rookie for making him look like a genius for letting him play.

Spencer seemed genuinely humble during his hot month, saying how he knew it was just a matter of time before he came down to earth. That was why the former replacement player was able to endear himself to his Yankee teammates. It's a good thing, because on a team that had veterans Strawberry, Tim Raines, and Chad Curtis available for duty in left field, it could have been a difficult situation for a rookie to suddenly be the player Joe Torre chose to pencil into the lineup almost every day. But every time you looked in the Yankee dugout after Spencer had hit another rocket over the center-field fence, you saw no resentment on any of those guys' faces. They were smiling broadly and looking dazzled by a remarkable hitting display. Bob "Hurricane" Hazle is one of the few players I can think of who came out of nowhere and was as hot for as long as Spencer. Back in 1957, Hazle played forty-one games and batted .403 as the Braves took the National League pennant. But Spencer hit more homers than Hazle and drove in the same number of runs in exactly half the number of at-bats. It was inevitable that he'd be compared to Roy Hobbs in *The Natural* and Joe Hardy in *Damn Yankees* because he had the best month ever by a nonfictional young player. Spencer was one more great story in the 1998 season.

Hazle was a one-year wonder, and as impressed as the Yankee brass were with Spencer they feared that might be his fate as well. That's why they would be in the market for a veteran left fielder in the off-season. Curt Simmons used to say, "Never judge a player by how he does in the spring or the fall." As good as Spencer was, he did it for only one month, and in a month when other teams were experimenting with their pitching staffs. So the jury is still out on whether Shane Spencer can hit anywhere near his September level for an entire season. If he fails as an everyday player, Spencer can take comfort in knowing that he at least hit well enough for a little over one month to have placed his name forever into baseball lore.

The Wild Card

If you are the I-was-in-the-wrong-place-at-the-wrong-time pitcher who had the dubious distinction of serving up Mark McGwire's sixty-second home run on September 8, you immediately started thinking that you must somehow do something mighty special to prevent that from being your sole legacy for the 1998 season. Perhaps Steve Trachsel was still contemplating this as he took the mound before 39,556 anxious fans at Wrigley Field on September 28, one day after the regular season had ended. As the Cubs' starter in the one-game play-off with the San Francisco Giants for the wild-card spot in the National League play-offs, the twenty-eight-year-old right-hander had the golden opportunity to pitch his team into the postseason for the first time since 1989. If he was on, he would not only finish the season with an excellent 15-8 record but also give fans something else to remember him by.

Trachsel had saved his best for last, no-hitting a hot Giants lineup for 6⅓ innings before pinch hitter Brent Mayne touched him with a single. Ahead 4–0 thanks to a two-run homer by forty-year-old Gary Gaetti in the fourth inning and a two-run pinch single by unlikely hero Matt Mieske in the fifth, the six-foot-four-inch Californian then departed. Like everyone else at Wrigley, he would hold on for dear life when the Cubs relievers almost blew a 5–0 lead in the ninth inning. The Giants scored three times before an overworked Rod Beck struggled, as has been his way, to save the victory for Trachsel. (Beck, with fifty-one saves, and Trevor Hoffman, with fifty-three saves for San Diego, had become the first single-season fifty-save twosome in baseball history.) The heavyset, mustachioed right-hander, whose frightening looks were at this point in his career as much of a weapon as his splitter, somehow finagled the dangerous Joe Carter into popping up with a man on in the final at-bat of a glorious career that was distinguished by clutch hits. The Cubs were victorious, 5–3, and reached the play-offs.

It was a thrilling ending to an extraordinary wild-card race in the National League that featured one team from each division. Until the last ten days of the season, there had been a year-long battle between the Cubs and New York Mets for the wild-card spot. But just when the two contenders began to run in place, Dusty Baker's Giants started to make up ground at an amazing clip. The Mets tanked, Brant Brown dropped a fly in left that cost the Cubs a game they had won, and suddenly the Giants had caught up and there was talk of the first three-way tie in baseball history. (The other one that could have been was in 1964: If the Cardinals had lost their final game there would have been a three-way tie for National League champion, but we won to finish one game up on the Reds and Phillies.) In fact, there would have been a three-way tie if the Mets had won their final game on a day when both the Cubs and Giants lost, but they dropped their fifth game in succession and, in shock, went home for the winter. If there had been a three-way tie, the Giants would have flown from Colorado, where they had concluded the regular season against the Rockies, to New York to play the Mets. If they would have won that game, they would have flown immediately to San Francisco to play the Cubs. Then if they would have beaten the Cubs for the wild-card championship, they would have had to fly to Atlanta to begin the divisional series against the Braves. The three games and three flights would have been scheduled for three days and eight time zones, which would have been beyond almost any player's capacity. As it turned out, the Giants would have gladly accepted such a mission impossible, instead of losing as they did in the play-off.

Many Cubs were happy besides Steve Trachsel and his relieved reliever Rod Beck. Of course, there was Sammy Sosa, who didn't improve on his 66 homers and major-league-leading 158 RBIs during the game but drilled two singles and scored two big runs in the Cubs' most important game of the season. Sosa had repeatedly told us that his entire season was directed not at beating Mark McGwire in the home-run race but at helping the Cubs reach the postseason—and his broad smile, blown kisses, and words of thanks to America in postgame interviews affirmed that this was true. Because the Cubs' victory over the Giants enabled him to complete his desired task of leading the Cubs into the postseason, while even McGwire couldn't lift the disappointing Cardinals into wild-card contention, Sosa would be voted the National League's Most Valuable Player in a landslide.

Also overjoyed to win the play-off was gifted first baseman Mark Grace, the only holdover from the Cubs' 1989 postseason team. He'd reached the postseason in only his second season and probably wondered, as did all Cubs fans, if he'd ever make it back. Grace, completing his eleventh .300 season, had the satisfaction of contributing a couple of hits in the big victory.

Although Brant Brown's contribution that day consisted of cheering from the dugout, it is safe to say that no one was happier about the Cubs' victory. In fact, many outsiders, including Yankees manager Joe Torre, admitted that they were rooting for the Cubs to win the wild card for Brown's sake. On September 23, the Cubs, who were once ahead 7–0 and coasting, were clinging to a 7–5 lead in the ninth inning against the Brewers in Milwaukee. The sure-handed Brown had gone to left field to play late-inning defense. Rod Beck pitched himself into a bases-loaded jam, but when Geoff Jenkins lofted a two-out fly toward the warning track in left, it appeared that the Cubs had survived a big scare. To the horror of Cubs fans, who had seen anything and everything snatch defeat from the jaws of victory over the years, Brown dropped the ball. By the time he picked it up and desperately threw it toward the infield, three runners had crossed the plate and the Brewers had pulled off a miraculous comeback victory. Afterward Brown broke down in the dugout while Chicago reporters clicked away on their old typewriters about such other ignoble blunders in baseball history as "Merkle's Boner" (also on September 23, in 1908), "Snodgrass's Muff" (which took place during the 1912 World Series), and Buckner's misplay in the 1986 World Series. There was no doubt that if the Cubs hadn't recovered from the loss and gone on to win the wild-card race, Brown would forever be linked to Fred Merkle, Fred Snodgrass, and Bill Buckner. No true baseball fan would wish such ignominy on any individual, particularly a youngster who was only a little confidence away from becoming an everyday player.

Although the wild-card race in the American League, in which Boston finished four games ahead of Toronto and seven games ahead of Anaheim, wasn't nearly as captivating as what took place in the National League, it too justified the existence of the wild-card format. Oddly, considering how popular baseball was in 1998, the only exciting race in the six divisions took place in the AL West, where Texas edged Anaheim by three games. So while the Yankees, Indians, Braves, Astros, and Padres ran away with their division titles, the wild-card races filled the void. The wild-card format has received many knocks, yet after the 1998 season its proponents can say with justification that it created a lot of excitement that baseball would not have had otherwise. Just like interleague play, the wild-card race is geared for the fans. I think its greatest advantage is that it establishes rivalries that haven't existed since both leagues went to divisional formats in 1969. Teams in each league always played one another, but since only the top teams in each division qualified for the postseason, a team from one division didn't care in the slightest about the records of its opponents in other divisions. A team wanted to win solely to help its own chances for reaching the postseason and not because it wanted to damage the other teams' chances. Since the advent of the wild card, every team cares what all the teams are doing in the other two divisions and goes tooth-and-nail with them because they could turn out to be their chief competitor for a play-off spot. Also significant is that fans, like the players, do some serious scoreboard watching—not just in the middle of September for teams in the same division but across the country. It is much more fun when every game matters. Last year, Mets fans had added reason to detest the Cubs and vice versa, and we were reminded of the intense rivalry these two teams had when they were in the same division. In future years, the wild card (and interleague play) will create or reestablish many more rivalries.

I don't think the wild card rewards mediocrity. It's true that it doesn't necessarily reward excellence, but it wasn't designed to do that. It was designed to spread things out, to have all teams share in the benefits of good play. The Red Sox won ninety-two games and the Cubs, with the win over San Francisco, won ninety, and I think that number of victories warranted their inclusion in postseason play. After all, division winners Cleveland and Texas won only eighty-nine and eighty-eight games, respectively. In 1997, the Florida Marlins, who were loaded with high-salaried players, won the world championship as a wild-card team. And this year's wild-card entries, the Cubs and Red Sox, had a number of pricey players. However, I think that the wild-card spot is a realistic goal for teams without astronomical budgets. Typically these would be overachieving teams that the scribes could call "the poor man's" or "the thinking fan's" champion. In the play-offs they would be the endearing underdogs who are cheered by fans of all the low-salaried teams that have fallen by the wayside. Until some of the owners of baseball's rich, elite teams agree to extensive revenue sharing, the wild-card spot may be the best and only goal for all the have-nots.

The American League Division Series

I think it was in the divisional play-offs that the 1998 New York Yankees turned the last of the cynics into converts who finally recognized that they deserved inclusion among the greatest teams ever. Because it was another example of the Yankees' winning any way they could, doing whatever was necessary to come out on top. They used little ball, longball, standout defense, and dominating pitching (a minuscule 0.33 ERA) to completely unravel a seemingly solid Texas Rangers team. The emotional Yankee players said they were inspired by Darryl Strawberry, who was in the hospital recovering from colon cancer surgery, but this team already had everything it needed to win.

The Yankees scored only nine runs and batted only .220 in the three-game series, but their victorious starters,

David Wells, Andy Pettitte, and David Cone, and relief corps led by Mariano Rivera allowed a strong-hitting Rangers team only one run and saddled them with an anemic .141 average. They made sure the Rangers never had a lead. In losing three successive games, the Rangers totaled only thirteen hits and managed just one walk in 21⅔ innings against the Yankee starters and four walks overall. And, as further evidence of the quality of the Yankees' pitchers, the Rangers' fearsome foursome of Juan Gonzalez (who had 157 RBIs for the year), Ivan Rodriguez, Rusty Greer, and Will Clark was a combined 4-for-44 with one run scored and one RBI (by Rodriguez).

In winning 2–0 and 3–1 in Yankee Stadium and 4–0 in Texas, the Yankees made the most of their few hits. In the two games in New York, all their runs were generated by the guys in the lower part of their unfairly strong lineup. In Game 1, the Yankees scored both their runs in the second inning after seventh-place hitter Jorge Posada drew a one-out walk against hard-throwing Todd Stottlemyre, the son of Yankees pitching coach Mel Stottlemyre. Then veteran Chad Curtis, Joe Torre's surprise choice as the opening game's left fielder over blazing-hot youngster Shane Spencer—Torre would invariably select the right guy to play this position throughout the postseason—doubled Posada to third. Next, Scott Brosius began what would be an amazing postseason for him with a single that scored Posada and sent Curtis to third. Then, as leadoff hitter Chuck Knoblauch struck out, Torre sent Brosius to second although he had as little chance of stealing safely against rifle-armed Ivan Rodriguez as Jean Valjean had of getting

away scot-free for swiping bread. But all Brosius intended
was to draw a throw, stop before he got to second base to
get in a run-down, and allow Curtis to race home with the
Yankees' second run. This gave David Wells enough of a
cushion to pitch with absolute confidence through eight
strong innings. That play gave me a rare chance as a
broadcaster to call attention to how the man on third on
that "double steal" will take a lead off third inside the baseline. That's the only time the lead is on the inside and the
reason for that, as the crafty Curtis understood, is to prevent the catcher from seeing third base and knowing how
far off the bag the runner is. If Rodriguez could have seen
how far Curtis was from the base, he might have thrown
behind him at third rather than throwing toward second
trying to get Brosius.

Now that the Yankees showed they could win with
"small ball," they then reverted to the home run, legacy of
the Bronx Bombers. All seven runs they scored in the second game at Yankee Stadium and in the only game at Texas
Stadium came via the round-tripper. Not surprisingly, the
first Yankee homer of the series was hit by Shane Spencer
in Game 2 off twenty-game winner Rick Helling, to give the
Yankees a 1–0 lead in the second inning. After starting Curtis in Game 1, Torre had inserted the team's hottest hitter
in left field and batted him seventh. And Spencer rewarded
Torre for his confidence by hitting his ninth homer of the
month in his first postseason plate appearance. Then, in
the fourth inning, Spencer singled to center and scored on
Brosius's two-run homer to right. The three runs were
more than enough for left-hander Andy Pettitte, who

yielded only three hits in seven innings and fanned eight Rangers one time each. Torre's decision to pitch Pettitte in the pivotal second game came under fire, but again the manager with the golden touch made the correct choice.

In Game 3, before 49,450 disillusioned Texas fans who wondered who had put a hex on the Rangers' bats, the Yankees scored all four runs in the sixth inning, when Paul O'Neill hit a solo homer and Shane Spencer—who else?—hit a three-run blast off Aaron Sele. After a three-hour, eighteen-minute rain delay, Cone, Graeme Lloyd, Jeff Nelson, and Rivera made the 4–0 score hold up. It had all been so easy. A good team had been swept by a Yankee club that wasn't even running on all cylinders. The Ranger players could only shake their heads as they watched their opponents celebrate their advancement to the ALCS. They had to doubt that any team in baseball had even a remote chance against such an awesome foe.

Although the Boston Red Sox were the wild-card entrant in the American play-offs, they won three more games than the Cleveland Indians, their opponent in the Divisional Series. Still, even with nineteen-game winner Pedro Martinez on the mound, it was a bit surprising that they took the first game of the series from the defending American League champions at Jacobs Field, especially by the convincing score of 11–3. I'm sure this game was particularly disconcerting to the Indians and their fans for two reasons. First, Martinez, who went seven strong innings, was far superior to the Tribe's young ace Jaret Wright, who couldn't make it out of the fifth inning. And second,

Boston's notorious one-two punch of Mo Vaughn and Nomar Garciaparra was even more frightening than expected. They alone drove in all eleven Red Sox runs, as Vaughn accounted for seven with a three-run homer in the first, a two-run homer in the sixth, and a two-run double in the eighth, and the young shortstop had a three-run homer in the fifth and a sacrifice fly in the eighth. The Indians would never shut down Garciaparra but they would win the series by keeping Vaughn from driving in another run and preventing Martinez from making another mound appearance.

The top of the first inning of Game 2 would go down as one of the more bizarre half-innings in 1998 and the turning point of the whole series. It began during a walk to the game's first hitter, Boston's Darren Lewis, when Indians starter Doc Gooden and home-plate umpire Joe Brinkman got into a heated argument over some highly questionable ball calls. To keep his pitcher in the game, Indians manager Mike Hargrove intervened, went at it with the short-tempered Brinkman, and was promptly thumbed from the game. With frayed nerves, Gooden returned to the mound, walked Lewis, walked John Valentin, and then gave up a double to Garciaparra. Lewis scored, but it appeared the relay throw had cut down Valentin at the plate. It looked like that on the replay and to Gooden, who was standing right there backing up home. Only Brinkman called Valentin safe, leading to more screaming and, without Hargrove around to protect him, Gooden's ejection by Brinkman. At the end of a year when umpires were heavily criticized for making so many bad calls in crucial situations—at the same time officials were under attack in the NFL—Brinkman had made an awful call and compounded his mistake by sending the best witness to the showers. This appeared to be the big break that Boston needed to jump ahead in the series two games to none. However, Brinkman's calls and ejections instead brought the moribund Indians back to life. They would score one in the first, five in the second, and one in the third as new pitcher Dave Burba held the Red Sox pretty much in check through the sixth inning, looking much more effective than Gooden, who wasn't getting the low-strike call. Eventually the Indians would prevail, 9–5. The hitting star was David Justice, who hit a decisive three-run homer off the Red Sox' short-lived starter Tim Wakefield, and had four RBIs on the day. As he first did with the Atlanta Braves, Justice showed that he is one of baseball's best big-game performers.

In Game 3 in Boston, the final score read Indians 4, Nomar Garciaparra 3. Garciaparra drove in the game's first run on a fielder's choice in the fourth inning and the game's final two runs on a two-run homer off Mike Jackson in the ninth inning. But in support of Charles Nagy, who gave up only four hits in eight innings, the Indians hit four solo homers. Jim Thome, who would have a remarkable postseason, Kenny Lofton, and Manny Ramirez went deep against Boston starter Bret Saberhagen, who gave up only one other hit in seven innings. Then Ramirez unloaded off Dennis Eckersley to lead off the ninth. Eckersley would retire the next three batters, including Thome on strikes, to complete the final inning of his career.

Game 4 was another nail-biter. Hard-throwing Bartolo Colon, who had the best stuff of the Indians' starters, and veteran lefty Pete Schourek were both in top form in stints that took them each into the sixth inning. Everybody in Boston had told manager Jimy Williams to pitch Pedro Martinez in this game, but in my opinion Williams was right to go with Schourek. Martinez could get only one more start, so why not pitch him in rotation with the proper rest? And how much better could he have done in seven innings than Schourek and right-hander Derek Lowe, who shut out the Indians on two hits. The game's only run had come in the fourth inning, when Garciaparra homered off Colon. With his team still holding a 1–0 lead, Jimy Williams gave his ace reliever Tom Gordon the ball to begin the eighth inning. The fans in Beantown felt the lead was safe because Gordon had ended the regular season with a major-league-record forty-three consecutive converted saves. But as several top relievers would learn in '98, pitching in the postseason is not the same as pitching in the regular season. Gordon found out the hard way, yielding singles to Kenny Lofton and Omar Vizquel, and then giving up the killer blow, a double to Justice that scored both runners. Did the year's most familiar phrase, "obstruction of Justice," cross his mind? The stunned Red Sox fans watched the rest of the game in near silence. The Indians were going to the ALCS. The Red Sox were pondering their future.

It was clear from this series that for them to have a chance to reach the play-offs again they would have to keep the Mo Vaughn–Nomar Garciaparra tandem that accounted for all five homers and seventeen of the eighteen

RBIs Boston accumulated in the four games. There was no way they could let Vaughn get away as a free agent. . . .

Perhaps my nicest memory of this series was looking down on the field and seeing Nomar Garciaparra leave the Red Sox dugout when the final out was made. Although he was certainly feeling bad about the loss, he went out on the field and turned to the hometown fans at Fenway. And this superstar, who had just hit three homers and driven in eleven runs in just four games, applauded *them*. It was a genuine gesture. In 1998 *class* was the operative word, and that's what Garciaparra is all about.

The National League Division Series

As the National League play-offs began, I considered the Houston Astros the most dangerous of the four teams. Atlanta and San Diego were also excellent teams, but in my opinion Houston had the best chance of stopping the Yankees juggernaut in the World Series. Led by Jeff Bagwell, Craig Biggio, Moises Alou, and Derek Bell, they had a high-octane offense that scored the most runs in the league. And they had Randy Johnson. The game's most intimidating left-hander was the one pitcher who had the potential to shut down the Yankees' predominantly left-handed lineup.

Johnson also had shown that he was nearly invincible against National League teams. The Astros, who had been swept by the Braves in the divisional series in '97, had acquired him from Seattle on July 31 in what was being hailed as the franchise's most significant trade in history because it was done with the postseason in mind. With Houston, Johnson was an extraordinary 10-1 against National League teams and was primed to be a dominating force in the National League playoffs as well. After watching him throw his 99-mph heater and unhittable sweeping slider for two months, Astros manager Larry Dierker relished having Johnson as his ace in a short series. Against the San Diego Padres, who had several key left-handed batters, he would have the luxury of going to his new lefty twice in the five-game divisional series. You don't assume anything in baseball, but who could have blamed Dierker if he figured that Johnson guaranteed him at least one victory and probably two? Nobody could have predicted that Johnson would pitch well enough to win, yet lose both starts.

Game 1, before over fifty thousand fans in the Astrodome, was the marquee matchup of the entire postseason. Johnson took his intimidating six-ten frame, mustache, and long locks to the mound to go against Kevin Brown. The right-hander was a fierce competitor who, in what would turn out to be his only year with the Padres, had gone 18-7 with a 2.38 ERA and 257 strikeouts (and only 49 walks) in 257 innings during the season. Moreover, in the previous year with the world champion Florida Marlins, Brown had been exceptional against the Giants and Braves in the National League play-offs. Brown had the credentials.

He also had the stuff. In 1997 with Florida, Brown

threw a no-hitter at the Giants and twice outdueled Greg Maddux in the NLCS, but it's hard to imagine him being more dominating than on this night. In eight shutout innings against a very tough Astros lineup, he gave up only two singles and struck out a play-off-record sixteen batters. Take nothing away from the Orioles' Mike Mussina, but when he struck out fifteen Indians in seven innings in the 1997 ALCS, he benefited from the four o'clock start in Cleveland that made it difficult for batters to pick up pitches. Brown had no such advantage. What makes Brown such an unusual strikeout pitcher is that he relies on balls that are down in the strike zone. Typically balls down in the strike zone are designed to have batters put the ball in play, not swing through them. What makes Brown's sinker so hard to hit is that its bottom falls out just like on a hard, heavy splitter.

Brown's feat was particularly impressive because it came against the most renowned strikeout pitcher. Johnson had nine strikeouts in his eight innings of work, but on this day Brown was superior. For five innings, the Big Unit held the Padres scoreless, but in the sixth inning Tony Gwynn, a left-handed batter who can hit anybody, anywhere, had a leadoff double and eventually scored the game's first run. Greg Vaughn, fresh from a fifty-homer season, gave the Padres insurance with a home run off Johnson in the eighth inning. The Astros would score an unearned run in the ninth against Trevor Hoffman. I'm sure Padres manager Bruce Bochy was tempted to let Brown pitch the final inning, but instead he brought in his closer, who had converted fifty-three of fifty-four save opportunities. I thought it was a gutsy move on his part, knowing when to stick to the script.

Interestingly, in Game 2 it was Hoffman who gave up an RBI single to Billy Spiers in the bottom of the ninth inning that gave the Astros a 5–4 victory and evened the series at one game each. It was a game in which Jeff Bagwell drove in three runs and their starter Shane Reynolds outpitched Andy Ashby, yet the Astros almost blew it when their own closer, Billy Wagner, yielded a dramatic two-out, two-run pinch homer to Jim Leyritz in the top of the ninth.

In Game 3, before 66,235 raucous fans in San Diego, Leyritz homered again, in the seventh inning off reliever Scott Elarton, for the winning run in the Padres' 2–1 victory. Kevin Brown, on three days' rest, pitched three-hit ball for 6⅔ innings before giving way to Dan Miceli, who got the victory. Trevor Hoffman pitched like he had all season, striking out the side in the ninth. Viewers from around the country must have been startled to watch the Padres being cheered on so vociferously, not by the staid southern California crowd that had always come to their games but by fans who would have seemed at home in the bleachers at Yankee Stadium or Wrigley Field. And was this really a San Diego baseball game, where a reliever with a goatee and intense eyes comes in from the bullpen to the ear-bursting strains of AC/DC's "Hell's Bells" and TREVOR TIME lights up on the scoreboard?

Because Brown went in Game 3, most conjectured that the Astros would prevail in Game 4, with Randy Johnson going against the less formidable Sterling Hitchcock. But nobody told Hitchcock that he was supposed to play second fiddle to the game's other left-hander that day. Like Johnson, he yielded only three hits in six innings, but he struck out eleven batters to Johnson's eight. Most significant, at the time both pitchers gave way to the bullpen, the Padres led 2–1, having just gone ahead on a throwing error by Astros third baseman Sean Berry. Johnson left the game with a 1.93 ERA for his two starts yet was going to suffer his second loss.

The Padres put the victory on ice by scoring four runs in the eighth inning, on a two-run pinch triple by John Vander Wal and a two-run homer by Wally Joyner. Joyner was in the lineup at first base despite Johnson's getting the start, with the Padres' hitting hero, Jim Leyritz, moving behind the plate. It was Leyritz who had put the Padres up 1–0 against Johnson in the fourth inning with another big homer. Leyritz will always be remembered for his game-tying homer for the Yankees off a slider thrown by the Braves' Mark Wohlers in the fourth game of the 1996 World Series. But with three homers and five RBIs in the four games while pinch hitting, playing first, and catching, he turned in a hitting performance reminiscent of pinch hitter/outfielder Dusty Rhodes's for the Giants against the Indians in the '54 World Series.

Finally, as the Padres crowd turned up the decibel level, Hoffman pitched a hitless ninth inning to nail down the decisive victory. The Astros, who batted only .182 for the series with no home runs and only three RBIs delivered by anyone other than Bagwell (who had four), had no hits against three Padres relievers over the final three innings and upped their strikeout total to thirteen. They had

Randy Johnson on their staff for two glorious months, but there had been no big payoff. Instead it was the rambunctious San Diego Padres who advanced to the NLCS.

Reaching the first round of the play-offs was a big deal for the Cubs. It had been nine years since they had been to the postseason, and in '98 it took a massive team effort just for them to squeak in by beating the Giants in a one-game play-off. Reaching the play-offs for the Atlanta Braves was old hat. It was almost like all they had to do to get into the postseason each year was to register for it during spring training, as if they were signing up at college for an extracurricular activity. Everyone knows it's not that easy, but each year they anticipated breezing through the divisional play-offs and then making it to the NLCS. In 1998 expectations were very high. Like the Yankees, the Braves had finished the regular season with seven consecutive victories, which gave them a franchise-record 106 wins. Everyone knows pitching wins short series and, once again, the Braves were loaded. In fact, on September 17, they had become the first team since the 1930 Washington Senators to boast five fifteen-game winners: John Smoltz, Tom Glavine, Greg Maddux, Denny Neagle, and Kevin Millwood.

As it turned out, the Braves didn't need all five starters to eliminate the Cubs. Their three Cy Young winners, Smoltz, Glavine, and Maddux, did the trick in three games, each with some strong relief from an unproven bullpen that was without troubled closer Mark Wohlers. In Game 1, before 45,598 fans and several thousand empty seats in Atlanta, Smoltz had a shutout until the eighth inning in the

Braves' 7–1 victory. Michael Tucker hit a two-run homer in the second inning off Cubs starter Mark Clark to give the Braves the lead and Ryan Klesko put the game away in the seventh inning with a grand slam off Matt Karchner. One good sign for the Cubs was that Sammy Sosa got two hits. It raised false hope that Sosa would break loose still another time with a torrent of home runs. He'd go hitless for the rest of the series.

Glavine, destined to win his second Cy Young Award after the season, held the Cubs to just three hits over seven innings in Game 2. But he gave up a run on a groundout in the sixth inning, and it appeared that Cubs starter Kevin Tapani would make that one run hold up. Tapani was cruising with a four-hit shutout through 8⅓ innings when Braves catcher Javy Lopez took a high fastball over the left-field fence to tie the game, 1–1. An inning later, Braves All-Star third baseman Chipper Jones won the game with an RBI single against Cubs reliever Terry Mulholland, who did himself in with a walk and a fielding error.

Lopez's homer is the hit that stands out in my mind from the series. A team's emotions are often a reflection of its fans and, for years, as David Justice had complained about when he was on the team, the Braves fans were annoyingly solemn and corporate when it came to getting behind their team. Consequently, the Braves players too often took on a business-as-usual attitude when they accomplished something. So it was great to see how visibly excited all the Braves were as they greeted Lopez after his game-saving heroics. I hadn't seen a Braves team show that much emotion since the 1995 World Series.

Bobby Cox sent Greg Maddux to the mound to pitch Game 3 at Wrigley Field—the right pitcher to entrust with securing any victory. Using his ace in the hole, Cubs manager Jim Riggleman countered with rookie sensation Kerry Wood, hoping he had sufficiently recovered from the arm woes that had ended his season in late August. Wood did an admirable job, holding the Braves to only three hits and striking out five in his five-inning stint. The one pitch he would have liked back was the one Maddux, one of the National League's best-hitting pitchers, clubbed into left-center for a double. Maddux moved to third on a ground-out and scored on a passed ball by Tyler Houston. The Braves led 1–0 and Maddux wouldn't lose his shutout until after the Braves rallied for five more runs off Terry Mulholland and a weary Rod Beck in the eighth inning. The final score was Atlanta 6, Chicago 2.

It's obvious why Atlanta won the series. In a combined 21⅔ innings, Smoltz, Glavine, and Maddux gave up only fifteen hits and four runs, walked just one batter, and struck out eighteen. Overall the Braves' staff had a 1.29 ERA and stifled the Cubs' most dangerous hitters: Sammy Sosa went two-for-eleven with no RBIs, Garry Gaetti went one-for-eleven with no RBIs, and Mark Grace went one-for-twelve with one RBI. As a team, the Cubs batted .181.

But I don't think the Cubs fans were too disappointed by how poorly their players fared against the Braves' outstanding pitchers. They were still grateful to Sosa and the rest of the Cubs for the regular season. I found it heartening to see how much excitement there was at Wrigley Field although almost everyone there knew that the Cubs weren't going to come back from a two-game deficit against the Braves in a five-game series, especially since Maddux was pitching in Game 3. Nevertheless, they were happy just to be in the park and to see their team play once more in '98. I think this was the first time I became aware that fans didn't want to see the '98 season end, because they were experiencing the game in all its glory. Baseball was again a habit for them, and habits are hard to break.

The American League Championship Series

The Indians lost their best chance to defeat the Yankees in the ALCS back on July 31, when they failed to swing a deal for Randy Johnson. The Yankees breathed a collective sigh of relief because Johnson would have given their most legitimate threat in the American League both a needed ace and a dominating left-hander who perhaps could silence the bats of key lefty swingers Paul O'Neill and Tino Martinez and force the Yankees' switch-hitters to bat from the right side. In the absence of Johnson, Indians manager Mike Hargrove would have to go with four right-handed starters, obviously giving the Yankees a significant edge.

In the first inning of Game 1 at Yankee Stadium, Hargrove must have wondered just how much more the Indians could have offered Seattle for Johnson. His choice to start the series, hard-throwing Jaret Wright, who had great success against the Yankees in the '97 Divisional Series, served up singles to the first four batters and eventually gave up five runs before being pulled after two-thirds of an inning. As Wright walked off the mound, he became the first Indian in the series to be victimized by unmerciful Yankee hecklers. As the ALCS moved back and forth between Yankee Stadium and Jacobs Field, passionate fans tried to outdo one another in the jeering department. Often it took precedence over what went down on the field in what would be a less than artful series with inconsistent play, shaky umpiring, and controversy.

Cheered by the home fans, David Wells was on cruise control, giving up only five hits in 8⅓ innings and holding the Indians scoreless until the ninth in the Yankees' 7–2 victory. As a tribute to Darryl Strawberry, recovering from colon cancer surgery, fans draped replicas of Darryl's number 39 jersey over the railing each time Wells recorded one of his seven strikeouts.

Having scored seven runs and totaled eleven hits in recording their eleventh consecutive victory, the Yankees probably thought they had broken out of the mild hitting slump that had plagued them against Texas in the Divisional Series. But in Game 2, they struggled again, coming up with only seven hits—no player had more than one—in twelve innings against Charles Nagy and six relievers. Their only run came on a score-tying RBI double in the seventh inning by Scott Brosius, who continued to drive in key runs.

Throughout the game, players complained about the

strike zone of home-plate umpire Ted Hendry. Eight Indians, including Jim Thome three times, and four Yankees
were called out on strikes on pitches that they insisted
were in a different time zone. But it was Hendry's call, or
noncall, on a bunt play in the top of the twelfth inning that
brought controversy to the series and determined the
game's outcome. As you may recall, Thome led off with a
single off Jeff Nelson and was replaced by pinch runner En-
rique Wilson. Travis Fryman, the next man up, then laid
down a bunt to the right side. Yankee first baseman Tino
Martinez played the ball as though he were not anticipat-
ing a bunt, moving away from first and then in, instead of
making a beeline for the ball. When he finally threw to second baseman Chuck Knoblauch covering first, Fryman
was almost on the bag. And since Fryman was running inside the baseline, Martinez couldn't make a clear throw.
The ball hit Fryman in the back just before he touched the
bag—just *after* according to some—and trickled past
Knoblauch and onto the outfield grass. First-base umpire
John Shulock called Fryman safe and Hendry did not sig-
nal interference to overturn that call—although, as I saw
it, it clearly was interference on Fryman for running inside
the baseline and preventing a clear throw. In fact, if interference isn't called on that play then they should change
the rule!

Ballplayers are taught to play the game, not umpire it,
but Knoblauch chose to argue with Shulock instead of
going after the errant throw. By the time he retrieved the
ball, Wilson was coming in to score the go-ahead run. The
Indians would tack on two more runs to make the final

score 4–1. The next day in the New York press and on call-in radio shows, Knoblauch was crucified for what the scribes called "brainlauch" and dubbed "BLAUCHHEAD" in bold-print headlines. It was insinuated that Knoblauch's decision to argue might result in the Yankees' failing to become champions. Feeling persecuted, Chuck felt he should issue a public apology. In my view, that was unnecessary. Fortunately, Joe Torre—as usual—managed to defuse the whole thing by standing by Knoblauch and saying he was entitled to an occasional misjudgment because of all the contributions he'd been making to the team's success.

I think Joe was sympathetic to why Knoblauch reacted as he did on the field. If Knoblauch had retrieved the ball and then argued the call, as everybody said he should have done, then he couldn't have sold his argument to Shulock. Only by standing his ground and arguing could Knoblauch show that he really believed that there was interference; if he automatically ran after the ball, then it would have had the opposite effect. He didn't want to give legitimacy to a play that should have been called dead the moment the ball struck Fryman's back. However, the umpires weren't willing to consider Knoblauch's sound argument—even in postgame interviews they stood by their call. The next day the media and enraged fans cried that the winning run scored because of Knoblauch's thoughtless play, but even if he had retrieved the ball the Indians would have had Wilson on third with no outs and it's extremely likely that they would have scored anyway.

In Game 3, before 44,904 hopped-up fans at Jacobs Field, the Indians rocked Andy Pettitte with four homers, two by Thome and one each by Manny Ramirez and Mark Whiten, and won easily, 6–1. Bartolo Colon, who was still throwing in the high nineties in the ninth inning, pitched a four-hitter to keep the Yankee batters mired in their slump. This was the first complete game pitched by a Cleveland Indian in the postseason since Bob Lemon did it in a losing effort in the 1954 World Series. Also, it was only the second time in 189 games that the Yankees were beaten by a pitcher who went the distance. The Indians were already thinking about how Colon would be the ideal starter if the series went to seven games. Unfortunately for them, it wouldn't go that far.

Joe Torre believes that the pivotal game in a seven-game series is Game 3, so he was understandably concerned when the Yankees lost. The Indians now had a two-games-to-one lead, the momentum with two straight victories, both Jim Thome and Manny Ramirez hot, and, because they had done it in '97, the mind-set that they could beat the Yankees. After the Yankees took the World Series title, it would be hard to sell the notion that a team that won 125 games during the season and eleven of thirteen in postseason play had one big game where everything was on the line, but Game 4 was such a game. It was crucial for the Yankees to win it because if they fell behind three games to one with one more game left to play in Cleveland, it would have been very difficult for them to come back and win the series. Realizing the significance of the game, David Wells went to Torre and volunteered to start Game 4 on four days' rest. However, Torre stuck with his game plan and gave Orlando Hernandez his first start of the postseason.

David Cone informed me that El Duque, new to the ways of American baseball, had expected to start Game 1 of the ALCS because the one-two-three men in the rotation had done away with Texas in three games and he assumed it was his turn. He was miffed that Torre went back to the beginning of the rotation to begin a new series, and I think it took some of Joe's unlimited diplomacy to get him to forget his anger and prepare himself mentally for when he did get the ball. Fortunately, Hernandez was able to do this, because, as fate would have it, he got his belated start in the Yankees' most important game of the year. In what George Steinbrenner would later call the best clutch pitching performance by a Yankee since Ron Guidry won the deciding game of the ALCS in 1978, Hernandez threw three-hit shutout ball for seven innings, completely mystifying the Indians hitters with his odd assortment of pitches, weird arm angles, and that unique high-legged, bent-knee delivery. The Cleveland fans tried to disrupt Hernandez with an unending stream of invective but, as Joe Torre laughed, "This guy came over on a raft—they're wrong if they think pressure will get to him." How Hernandez was that effective after a lay-off of more than two weeks was testament to his iron will and talent. I think that even people close to the game still don't fully appreciate the enormity of Hernandez's accomplishment.

Meanwhile, the Yankees scored three times off the right-handed Dwight Gooden. Left-handed Paul O'Neill hit a first-inning homer and left-handed Tino Martinez and switch-hitter Chili Davis, batting from the left side, drove in runs in the fourth inning with back-to-back hits. They would score their final run, in their important 4–0 victory, in the ninth inning off Dave Burba. Mike Stanton and Mariano Rivera, who was convincing everybody that he was in top form despite several shaky outings at the end of the year, dispatched the Indians in the final two innings. For the game, the Indians had only four hits, three by shortstop Omar Vizquel. The heart of their order, David Justice, Manny Ramirez, and Jim Thome, were a combined 0-for-10 and struck out six times. As Hernandez watched the relievers secure a victory, he must have felt such satisfaction. He had shown everybody in America, including his teammates, his manager, and the owner who had signed him to a risky contract, why he had been a hero in Cuba when he pitched the national team to many big victories. He had just pitched the Yankees to victory in their only must-win game of the year.

The Yankees came out with renewed vigor in Game 5, scoring three runs in the first inning off starter Chad Ojea, with leadoff hitter Knoblauch getting hit by a pitch and O'Neill and Davis again providing key hits. An RBI single by O'Neill in the second inning sent Ojea to the showers. This time Jaret Wright, pitching in long relief, was effective. He yielded only two hits and one run over six innings, but by the time he came into the game, the outcome had been decided. Understandably, Yankee starter David Wells was stung by insensitive remarks by loud fans about his recently deceased mother as he tried to warm up prior to the game. He almost squandered the runs the Yankees scored in their half of the first by giving up a leadoff homer to Kenny Lofton and, after two singles and a wild pitch, a sacrifice fly to Manny Ramirez. But he escaped the first inning with a 3–2 lead and settled down. He would give up only four more hits in his final 6⅓ innings of work, and the sole run came on a homer to Thome, who can hit lefties as well as righties. "I'm probably prouder of this effort [by David] than any of his others," Joe Torre was later quoted in *Sports Illustrated.* "Because of when it happened, what it meant to us and how he didn't panic." Wells was reluctant to leave the game when Torre decided to bring in right-handed pitchers to face a string of right-handed Indian batters in the eighth inning. He could relax only after Rivera got the final out in the 5–3 victory and recorded his third save of what was turning out to be a fantastic post-season for the reliever, who had been maligned since his failure in last year's Divisional Series.

Significantly, David Justice wasn't in the Indians' lineup against Wells. Apparently Justice had told Hargrove that he wouldn't be offended if he were placed low in the batting order against the good left-hander. Hargrove said he thought this meant Justice was trying to find a way out of the lineup entirely, so he stuck Justice on the bench for the entire game. Justice did not look happy and I don't blame him. The next day he would call a press conference to assure everyone that he would never have asked out of a game. Was there an inJustice? Based on his track record, I'd say Justice never would bail out of a big game no matter who was on the mound. He always has been a big-time player and it was unfortunate that he wasn't in the lineup for such a pivotal game. I don't know what went on between Justice and Hargrove in what seemed akin to a marital spat. I just know that Joe Torre wouldn't have allowed anything similar to develop into a volatile, public issue—especially not during the later stages of the ALCS.

The Indians' season ended two nights later in Yankee Stadium, where fans gave their players something extra to think about by decorating the ballpark with pictures of Uzis and other machine guns. Justice had deflected criticism of Indians fans by saying that in Yankee Stadium the fans said and did everything but carry Uzis. This was the response. For the fifth time in the six games, the resourceful Yankees scored in the first inning, coming up with two early runs as four batters from the left side provided three hits and a sacrifice fly. Then everyone got into the act. They scored an unearned run in the second inning and in the third inning—after a bad call (by Ted Hendry, again) on a force play at second base kept the Yankees' inning alive—Scott Brosius continued to amaze by tagging Charles Nagy with a three-run homer over the center-field fence. The Indians starter departed with the Indians trailing 6–0. With David Cone on the mound for the Yankees, hopes dimmed for the Tribe. But they did show surprising resilience by coming back to score five runs off the tiring Cone in the fifth inning to make the score 6–5.

The big blow was a grand slam by Jim Thome, who was putting on a big show after missing a month late in the season with a broken hand. I remember that Pete Rose used to pull me aside and point toward George Foster and say, "That guy is a *slugger*." That's the word to describe Thome, who hit four homers (with eight RBIs) against the Yankees and six in the postseason. It got to the point where you'd give him a fifty-fifty chance of homering each time he came to the plate. What a slugger!

Thome put the Indians back in the game, but they couldn't get even. Yankee middleman Ramiro Mendoza pitched three brilliant innings of shutout ball, yielding only one hit and causing Yankee haters across the country to protest, "Just how many great pitchers does this team have?!" By the time Mendoza left, the Yankees were comfortably in front 9–5, the final score. They came up with the three additional runs in the sixth inning. After Vizquel, the game's best fielding shortstop, had a throwing error on Brosius's grounder—his first miscue in 46 postseason games—you knew the opportunist American League East champs would take advantage. The big blow was by Derek Jeter to deep right with two men on base. Ramirez climbed the wall to try to rob Jeter of a homer, but his valiant effort was wasted because he had badly misjudged the flight of the ball. While Ramirez went upward, the ball came down at the base of the wall. Both runners scored. Jeter was credited with a triple on Ramirez's misplay and later scored the Yankees' final run on Bernie Williams's RBI single. With his fifth RBI, Williams tied O'Neill for second place on the Yankees in the ALCS, one behind Brosius.

Fittingly, Mariano Rivera closed out the game and the series with one inning of perfect relief. For the ALCS, he pitched 5⅔ innings of hitless baseball, giving up only one walk and striking out five. Almost forgotten was the home run he had given up to Sandy Alomar in Game 4 of the '97 Divisional Series that led to, with another loss the following day, the Yankees' early elimination. Rivera had shown his mettle and was vindicated in everyone's eyes.

After having nearly beaten the Marlins in the 1997 World Series, the Indians were optimistic about capturing another world title on the fiftieth anniversary of their last one, against the old Boston Braves in 1948. Perhaps they felt they should have won the ALCS after taking a two-games-to-one edge, but I think their winning those two games against this Yankee team was the biggest "upset" of the postseason, on par with the Padres' victories over the Astros and Braves in the National League play-offs. Maybe after watching the Yankees dispose of the Padres in four straight games to give them eighteen wins in twenty games dating back to the regular season, the Indians realized it was a real accomplishment just to win those two games. Realistically, it would have been most difficult for this Indians team, without Randy Johnson, to prevent the Yankees from winning their thirty-fifth American League pennant.

The National League Championship Series

The Atlanta Braves have deservedly been called the "Team of the Nineties" on the basis of their record seven consecutive division titles and three World Series appearances. However, their inability to win more than their one world title in 1995, despite having a plethora of high-priced talent, has taken some of the luster off their achievement. In 1998, they set franchise records when they won 106 games, slugged 215 home runs, made only 91 errors, and had five 15-game winners. So they went into the NLCS feeling extremely optimistic. John Smoltz, in fact, called this the best of the Braves teams he'd been on. After the NLCS was over he was at a loss to explain his team's defeat by the upstart Padres. I think what the NLCS did was reveal a lot of weaknesses that the Braves were able

to cover up during the season. Specifically: Kerry Ligtenberg wasn't ready to replace the disabled Mark Wohlers as
the closer; Bobby Cox had no down-and-dirty jack-of-all-
trades second baseman like Mark Lemke to turn the double play, bat second, and be a spark plug; and Cox's lineup
against left-handers was weak because he had no high-
caliber right-handed batters to platoon with Ryan Klesko
and Michael Tucker.

The NLCS also affirmed that emotion is the intangible
element that often determines who wins in the postseason. Emotion has never been the strong suit of a team that
revolves around three low-key cerebral pitchers and
whose fans too often take their winning team for granted.
The Padres, on the other hand, followed the emotional
leads of two intense players, pitcher Kevin Brown and
third baseman Ken Caminiti, and the player who has more
fun than anyone just playing the game, Tony Gwynn. The
Padres fans came to Qualcomm Stadium in droves to show
management that the team had a strong enough fan base
to warrant the construction of another stadium. They
never hid their love for their team.

The NLCS was written up in various newspapers as a
battle between Padres ace Kevin Brown and the Braves'
vaunted threesome of Smoltz, Tom Glavine, and Greg
Maddux. They were, after all, four of the six starting
pitchers in the league with an ERA below 3.00. However,
Andy Ashby was only slightly behind Smoltz's 2.90 ERA
with a 3.34 ERA, and when they hooked up in Game 1 at
Turner Field in Atlanta, he was Smoltz's equal. Ashby,
who has such extension that it seems like the ball is on

top of the batter the moment he releases it, gave up a third-inning homer to Andruw Jones but only four other hits and no more runs in seven impressive innings. Smoltz relinquished an RBI single to Tony Gwynn in the fifth but headed into the eighth inning with a three-hitter. However, a leadoff double by Ruben Rivera, the second cousin of Yankees closer Mariano Rivera, ended Smoltz's night. John Rocker, perhaps a closer-in-waiting, and Dennis Martinez finished the inning, in which Rivera scored on the first of two errors in the inning by Andres Galarraga, a usually reliable first baseman.

Trevor Hoffman came in to pitch the ninth for the Padres. He had his invincible demeanor and a magnificent change-up, but couldn't protect the 2–1 lead. After a walk and a single, Andruw Jones knotted the game with a sacrifice fly. The start of the game had been delayed by more than two hours by rain, and not only had the downpour dampened the spirits of the 42,217 Braves fans who bought tickets, but it resulted in about two-thirds of them going home before the game's conclusion. (Unlike Joe Torre, I think the first game is the most important in a short series.) Braves reliever Kerry Ligtenberg yielded a home run to a limping Ken Caminiti, who took his 3-1 fastball over the center-field fence in the top of the twelfth to give the Padres a 3–2 victory. Oddly, with two outs in the bottom of the tenth, Padres manager Bruce Bochy replaced Hoffman, who had fifty-three saves during the year, with Donne Wall, who had one. Wall walked a batter but did record the final out for his first and only postseason save in 1998.

The following night, under clear Atlanta skies, Glavine faced off against Brown, the Braves' nemesis in the '97 NLCS. Brown was wearing his angry, you-will-not-beat-me look, with eyes that couldn't have been more chilling. At times he'd disdainfully turn his back on batters he struck out, making his carriage even more demonstrative. Glavine managed to stick with Brown in a scoreless tie for five innings, although he wasn't getting strike calls from Larry Poncino on the pitch just off the outside corner, his bread-and-butter pitch. But in the sixth, Chris Gomez, Brown, and leadoff hitter Quilvio Veras strung together two-out singles against Glavine to put the Padres up 1–0, and his night was over. It could have been more damaging, but Brown was thrown out trying to advance to third on Veras's hit to center. He was so intent on reaching safely that he dove into the base. Don't think that something like that from a pitcher isn't inspiring to the whole team. However, that was the last thing on Bochy's mind—he was just relieved that Brown hadn't hurt himself. Because with Brown back on the mound and pitching as he had been, even a one-run lead would hold up. Brown went on to pitch a three-hit shutout with eleven strikeouts. After his third appearance in the postseason, he had an impressive line: 23⅔ innings, 8 hits, 1 earned run, 32 strikeouts. For icing, he got his second hit of the game and scored as the Padres rallied for two runs in the ninth off Odalis Perez to make the final score 3–0.

Most teams who lose the first two games of a best-of-seven series at home would begin to panic. But the Braves saw no need to lose their cool because they had four-time

Cy Young winner Greg Maddux waiting in the wings to pitch Game 3. And Sterling Hitchcock, his pitching opponent in the first game in San Diego, had an ERA during the season more than double that of Maddux, the league leader. Hitchcock had the right attitude about going against the decade's best pitcher: "There's no pressure on me—I'm not expected to win." The left-hander, who had been traded by both the Yankees and Mariners, wasn't as sharp as when he won the final game of the Padres-Astros Divisional Series, but he didn't have to be because he was left-handed. A left-hander can get by with less in the major leagues because batters aren't as familiar with them and because their pitches have natural movement. And against the Braves, Hitchcock faced a weaker lineup, minus strong left-handed bats Klesko and Tucker, than Bobby Cox would have fielded against a right-handed pitcher. He gave up only three hits in five innings and only a single run in the top of the fifth.

Maddux usually protects a 1–0 lead as if it were the crown jewels, but he faltered with two outs in the bottom of the fifth when Hitchcock grounded a single to left, Steve Finley doubled, and Ken Caminiti singled up the middle. Suddenly the Padres were ahead 2–1 and Maddux was lifted for a pinch hitter in the top of the sixth. Hitchcock got four innings of solid relief by Donne Wall, Dan Miceli, Randy Myers, and Trevor Hoffman, who went the final 1⅓ innings and struck out three, giving up one hit. For the third straight game, all losses, Bobby Cox used three relievers and had only two emerge unscathed. Rudy Seanez didn't pitch well in giving up the Padres' third and fourth runs in the ninth inning, but it should be pointed out that in his brief time on the mound there were two errors and a passed ball.

Atlanta was now down 3–0 with the realization that no team had ever come back from that deficit in postseason play. In fact, no team down that far had ever taken the series to a sixth game. But in San Diego, Atlanta won Games 4 and 5, which had remarkably similar story lines. In both games, the Padres took early 2–0 leads but the Braves came back to tie with single runs in the fourth and sixth innings. In Game 4, the Padres took a 3–2 lead in the sixth inning, when Leyritz homered off starter Denny Neagle; in Game 5, the Padres took a 4–2 lead in the sixth inning, when John Vander Wal smacked a two-run homer off Smoltz. In Game 4, the Braves rallied for six runs (including a Lopez homer to chase Hamilton and a grand slam by Galarraga) in the seventh inning and won 8–3; in Game 5, the Braves rallied for five runs in the eighth inning, and won 7–6.

Both games were highly entertaining, but Game 5 was much more intriguing from a strategic standpoint. Braves right fielder Michael Tucker was prominent in two particularly compelling moments. It was Tucker who knotted the game with a sixth-inning single, but it should be pointed out that Tucker was batting eighth, there were two outs, and the lone runner, Andruw Jones, was on second after a steal. You rarely see Bruce Bochy show emotion, but as Jones came around to score the tying run, our cameras caught him slamming his hat on the bench. I know that he was second-guessing himself for not having ordered Ashby to give Tucker a free pass and pitch to Smoltz. Smoltz is a good-hitting pitcher but he's not nearly as good a hitter as Tucker.

With two outs in the seventh inning, Bochy brought in Kevin Brown. The pennant was on the line and, with a 4–2 lead, Bochy hoped, I believe, to use his ace starter through the eighth inning and then bring in Trevor Hoffman to get the save. I think it was a smart move, like when Tommy Lasorda used starter Orel Hershiser, who was unhittable at the time, to get the final out in the fourth game of the 1988 NLCS against the Mets. But after getting out of the seventh inning, Brown had trouble in the eighth. Klesko walked and Lopez reached on an infield hit. Then with one out and the tying runs on base, the left-handed Michael Tucker, who had already driven in two runs, strode to the plate representing the go-ahead run. We mentioned on the air that Tucker, a low-ball hitter, would be extremely dangerous against a tired sinkerball pitcher like Brown. The circumstances had changed and perhaps it was time to take out Brown and bring in a left-hander, either Randy Myers or Mark Langston. But Bochy stuck with Brown, respecting his competitive fire and probably knowing that his ace gave up the fewest home runs per nine innings of any starter in the major leagues. But throw the stats out the window, because Tucker went down and got hold of a Brown sinker and drove it over the wall in right field. Gwynn slumped against the fence in right, Brown clutched his head on the mound, and Tucker merrily circled the bases, having put his team up 5–4. The Braves added a couple more runs in the inning against Wall, which served them well because the Padres would score twice more against Ligtenberg when Greg Myers hit a two-run pinch homer with nobody out in the ninth.

That's when Bobby Cox followed Bochy's lead and brought in Maddux. Later Maddux said he had no idea how to act out there in the unfamiliar role of closer. As you might expect of the Professor, he caught on fast. He struck out pinch hitter Greg Vaughn (whose leg injury had kept him out of the lineup) and got Veras on a grounder to second. But things got a bit hairy when Maddux uncharacteristically walked Steve Finley. Maddux well understood that it wasn't a good idea to put the potential tying run on base with Tony Gwynn, an eight-time National League batting champion, on deck. What a way for the game to end: the decade's best pitcher facing the decade's best hitter. Good pitching is supposed to negate good hitting, but Gwynn had studied Maddux so much that he had managed to bat around .450 against him lifetime. It was an extremely tense situation that ended not with a bang but with a whimper. Gwynn grounded out to first to end a marvelous game. Maddux had been pitching in the majors since 1986 and in 1998 won his two hundredth game, but this was his first save ever!

The Braves returned to Atlanta with confidence. They had even picked up some emotion playing in front of the huge, vocal crowds in San Diego. And for Game 6, the 50,998 fans at Turner Field showed anything but complacency, perhaps after seeing how much impact the Padres crowd had had on their team. Apparently they liked the

Braves on those rare occasions when they were the underdogs. Unfortunately, lefty Sterling Hitchcock returned to the mound for San Diego, and Ryan Klesko and Michael Tucker returned to the Atlanta bench, leaving behind a lesser Braves batting order. (The Braves' biggest power threat, Andres Galarraga, went 0-for-3 to finish the NLCS at 2-for-21.) Hitchcock shut out the Braves on two hits over five innings, and four relievers, including Hoffman in the ninth inning, shut them out for the final four innings. Again Tom Glavine pitched when his team was shut out. He also took a shutout into the sixth inning but then gave up five runs, only two of which were earned. That took the crowd out of the game and the passion out of the Braves players.

The biggest play of the game came with the left-handed-batting Hitchcock at the plate. We pointed out on the air that left fielder Danny Bautista was playing too deep to guard against balls hit the opposite way. Sure enough, Hitchcock stroked a low liner the opposite way over the infield and Bautista, who got a bad break, charged in and had the ball go off his glove as he leaned over awkwardly. He later said that he'd lost the ball in the lights. But in this game situation, that ball has to be caught. Instead the error—an error with the glove that resulted from an error in positioning—brought in two more Padres runs and put the game out of reach. The Padres would score once more in the inning to make the final score 5–0.

Again in defeat, the Braves started to wonder what went wrong and to reevaluate their team. They immediately started to ponder what it would take to reach the World Series in 1999. The Padres wouldn't have to wait that long. Even during their wild victory celebration, the players were thinking about getting on a plane and heading north to New York, where they would play in the 1998 World Series against the Yankees.

The World Series

"Keep the Faith." That had been the San Diego Padres' mantra during the 1998 season, and those words had even more meaning as they prepared to play the seemingly invincible New York Yankees in the World Series. The Padres had won 98 games during the season but that was fourth best in the majors, so it had become their mission to knock off the other three teams during their march to a world title. In succession they surprised the Astros, who had won 102 games, in the Divisional Series, and the Atlanta Braves, proud owners of a franchise-record 106 victories, in the National League Championship Series. Now they had to pull off just one more upset to be champions. And what could be more satisfying than to win the World Series by beating the team everyone was calling one of the greatest ever, the New York Yankees, winners of an American League–record 114 games during the season and 121 games overall?

No team that had won one hundred games or more in the past decade had gone on to win the World Series, but I'm sure the Padres realized that these Yankees were an entirely different breed from those upset victims. They were a relentless foe who seemed to have a foolproof game plan for winning every game. They had won fourteen out of their last sixteen games going back to the regular season, and it almost seemed as if they were now incapable of tasting defeat. Some teams forget how to win— these Yankees forgot how to lose. And when opposing managers, including the Padres' Bruce Bochy, looked at the scouting reports, they realized that the '98 Yankees had no real weaknesses, no chinks in their armor.

The Padres probably would have been better off if they could have started the World Series in the friendly confines of Qualcomm Stadium, because it is not easy to come into Yankee Stadium for the first time and simply play ball. I remember first seeing the Stadium when the Cardinals played the Yankees in the '64 World Series, and I felt like I was on holy ground and the Stadium was a great basilica. And, naturally, the ghosts of Ruth, Gehrig, and other Yankee legends were wandering about. Surprisingly, Tony Gwynn had never been to Yankee Stadium before and he made a point of visiting it a day in advance of the Series so he wouldn't be overwhelmed on game day. Tony, a really genuine guy (besides being a hitting machine), decided to be just like the typical fan and, with his sixteen-year-old son in tow, took the Lexington Avenue train from midtown up to the 161st Street station in the Bronx. They went past the ticket booths along the outside of the stadium and avoided the scalpers, who seemed to materialize out of nowhere. Tony didn't need a ticket, now, did he? Once inside, Tony and his son strolled across the infield diamond and the outfield grass to see the plaques out in Monument Park and read about deceased Yankee greats, from the Babe and the Iron Horse to Mickey Mantle and Roger Maris. A devotee of baseball history, Tony took it all in that first day, but, not satisfied, on game day insisted on meeting Bob Shepard, Yankee Stadium's renowned public-address announcer. Now that's showing respect to a stadium and its personnel. Shepard asked Tony if he wanted to introduce him in a certain way, but Tony said, "Nope. *Your* way's just fine." That Gwynn, returning to World Series play for the first time in fourteen years, would have a terrific series despite assorted leg and Achilles problems is, to me, another of the great stories of 1998.

Gwynn is such a classy guy that I hope the Yankee Stadium crowd was more lenient toward him than they were to other Padres players and personnel. Pitching coach Dave Stewart came away with the impression that Yankee fans believe anybody in a Padres uniform has the last name Sucks. That was one of the kinder words used. Fortunately, ballplayers are thick-skinned enough to laugh at such things, and the Padres didn't show any signs of being intimidated by those overzealous fans (who were a small minority) with an uncanny knowledge of expletives. Or by New York City, or by the majestic ballpark.

David Wells started for New York in the World Series opener, coming into the game with a 7-1 record and 2.63 ERA in ten postseason starts, including wins in the opening games of the '98 Divisional Series and ALCS. It would be the last game he would pitch as a Yankee. His opponent was Kevin Brown, who had been magnificent in the play-offs. It wasn't known by us in the broadcast booth (or by anyone else, for that matter) that Brown, along with Andy Ashby and other Padres, had been struck by a mysterious, energy-sapping virus. All game long he was fatigued but kept pitching. As he always did, baseball's most tenacious pitcher reminded me of Jack Morris when he threw a masterful ten-inning 1–0 shutout for Minnesota against Atlanta in the seventh game of the 1991 World Series.

What no one realized until after the game was how badly Brown was hurt in the second inning on a line-drive infield single by Chili Davis. The ball hit him squarely on the left shin, and in order to withstand the pain and stay in the game, Brown had to subtly alter his pitching motion. Fortunately, Brown was used to throwing from various angles anyway (like David Cone), but before he'd had time to adjust he had issued walks to Tino Martinez and Jorge Posada and yielded a two-run double to ninth-place hitter Ricky Ledee. The Yankees led 2–0.

Joe Torre again manipulated his left-field placement with aplomb and inserted the young Ledee as his left fielder rather than Tim Raines, Shane Spencer, or Chad Curtis. It was perhaps his most unexpected and sensible move. Only on the postseason roster because of Strawberry's illness, Ledee batted just seventy-nine times all year but was now starting in the first game of the World Series—and producing. (As Dinah Washington used to sing: "What a difference Ledee makes.") Torre went with Ledee to put another left-handed bat in the lineup against Brown and also because of Ledee's speed and range in left field. In the first inning, Torre's decision immediately paid dividends when Ledee charged the ball so quickly on Tony Gwynn's hit-and-run single that Quilvio Veras, who had walked, had to stop at second. There would have been runners on first and third with no outs, and it's likely a run would have scored. But without a runner on third, Wells pitched out of the jam. That was an important moment in the game.

By the third inning, Brown seemed to have found his groove. Not so with David Wells. In the top of the third, Greg Vaughn launched a Wells pitch over the fence in right-center with a man on board to tie the game at 2–2. Then, in the fifth inning, Gwynn, who later told me he had calculated that Wells would throw him an inside fastball, hit an inside fastball to never-never land—even Gwynn's greatest admirers thought he'd *never* hit a baseball that far. He smoked Wells's pitch off the façade below the upper deck in right field. Following Gwynn's mighty two-run blast, Vaughn hit his second home run off Wells, this time to left field, to make the score 5–2, Padres. Vaughn was thrilled to put on this power display in Yankee Stadium because in 1997 he had been traded by the Padres to the Yankees for Kenny Rogers, only to have the Yankees renege on the deal when they decided Vaughn was damaged goods because of a bad shoulder. Instead they traded Rogers to Oakland for Scott Brosius and Vaughn stayed put and smashed fifty homers for the Padres. (All three teams benefited.)

Kevin Brown holding a three-run lead heading into the seventh inning could be called a sure thing. But he was wearing out from the virus and his leg was aching. Also, he was pitching against a team that always found ways to pull out comebacks, no matter what the score was and who was pitching. Fans would ask, "How will the Yankees win today?" and soon they'd answer, "Ah, here's a new way." Against Brown and the Padres, the Yankee comeback was unlike anything we'd seen. Brosius opened the inning by grounding out, but Posada singled to right. Ledee's double in the second inning made Brown pitch to him more carefully in the seventh. Brown, completely out of gas, was reluctant to challenge Ledee again and tried to get the youngster to bite at pitches off the plate. But Ledee showed the poise of a veteran and took four straight balls. The walk to Ledee was so critical because it brought Bochy out to make a pitching change. It was generally conceded that if the Padres were to have a chance to win the Series, Brown would have to win his starts, yet now Bochy was removing him from the game with the potential tying run at home plate. Many people would criticize Bochy for having a quick hook, but none of us knew about Brown's physical problems that night or that, before the inning started, he had actually told his manager to watch him closely.

Bochy didn't second-guess himself for taking out Brown, but he would for bringing in Donne Wall instead of Joey Hamilton. Wall had done a good job for Bochy all year, but in this situation, when Bochy wanted a grounder, he brought in a fly-ball pitcher instead of a sinkerballer. Unfortunately for the Padres, Wall got his fly ball. On a 2-0 count, he threw a high fastball over the middle of the plate and Chuck Knoblauch jumped all over it, sending it soaring over the left-field fence to tie the game. Brown's gutsy performance had gone for naught, and suddenly the stunned visiting team was holding on, hoping that their inconsistent middle relievers could stymie the potent Yankees. They couldn't. As crushing as Knoblauch's blow was, the worst was yet to come.

Derek Jeter, the next batter, singled to center. With several left-handed batters and switch-hitters due up, Bochy then yanked the shocked Wall and brought in veteran left-hander Mark Langston, who was several years past being one of the game's best pitchers. Langston got the tough O'Neill to fly out, but Jeter went scurrying to second on a wild pitch to Bernie Williams. With first base open, Langston intentionally walked the American League's batting champion but then he unintentionally walked Chili Davis to load the bases. That brought up the left-handed Tino Martinez, who was experiencing his usual postseason woes but was very dangerous nonetheless. Langston pitched him carefully. With the count 2-2, Langston threw the pitch he wanted, a ball that went over the plane of the plate and dipped beneath the knees. A ball that low is often called a strike in the National League, but American League umpire Rich Garcia called it ball three and Langston's face expressed anguish. That pitch was too close for me to call and too close for Martinez to have taken it with two strikes. With the count 3-2, Langston knew he had to bring the ball up or force in the go-ahead run. Martinez knew that too and was sitting on Langston's fastball. His mammoth grand slam into the right-field stands sent shock waves through the stadium and plunged Langston and the entire Padres team into despair. The Yankees scored seven in the seventh and showed everyone once again how they could make an impossible comeback. They would go on to win Game 1 by a score of 9–6, a vital game the Padres thought they had secured.

As I've said several times, what made the '98 Yankees so difficult to beat was that they were capable of winning in every kind of way. In Game 1 they won with a late-inning comeback. In Game 2, they won by pouring it on in the early innings. In the first inning they parlayed four singles, a walk, a stolen base, and a throwing error by hobbled third baseman Caminiti into three runs. In the second inning, they scored three more times on Jeter's RBI single and Williams's two-run homer. Ledee's RBI double in the third inning upped the lead to 7–0 and knocked the ill but valiant starter Andy Ashby from the box. Their final two runs would come on a two-run homer by Posada in the fifth inning. With that blast the Yankees became the first team in World Series history to score at least nine runs in the first two games. Yankee starter Orlando Hernandez benefited from the onslaught. A year after his younger stepbrother Livan Hernandez shone while pitching the Florida Marlins to a World Series victory over Cleveland, El Duque proved that grace under pressure was a family trait. Before enjoying a celebratory cigar (Costa Rican, not Cuban, he insisted) in the clubhouse, he pitched seven strong innings, giving up six hits and one run while fanning seven in the Yankees' 9–3 victory.

The Padres were happy to be leaving hostile, surreal Yankee Stadium and returning to sunny San Diego. Those who had become ill would have a chance to recover with a little home cooking. And all the players were eager to see their own true-blue Padres fans. These fans held tailgate parties, root-root-rooted for the home team, and rarely said a nasty word to their opponents. More than 64,000 filled Qualcomm Stadium for Game 3, and their presence had a soothing effect on the Padres.

As mentioned, Joe Torre considers the third game to be the most important in a seven-game series, and that's why he had David Cone slated in that spot whether the Yankees' opponent would be the Braves or the Padres. For one thing, Cone would benefit from warm weather. In Game 3, Cone proved again that he is a money pitcher by tossing no-hit ball for five innings. But the score stood at 0–0 because Sterling Hitchcock was pitching a gem of his own. I think that a good left-handed pitcher had a better chance of beating the Yankees than even a great right-handed pitcher like Kevin Brown. And Hitchcock, who was tremendous in the NLCS, proved to be highly effective on the mound. He also did his job with the bat, ending Cone's no-hit bid with a single to lead off the bottom of the sixth. He would later score on Gwynn's single to put the Padres ahead 1–0. The Padres would up their lead to 3–0 before the inning ended, as Paul O'Neill made a costly throwing error and Caminiti had a sacrifice fly.

The Padres were up by three runs after six innings, as

they had been in Game 1, but Hitchcock may have exhausted himself by pitching out of a bases-loaded jam in the top of the sixth inning and running the bases in the bottom of the inning. An indication of this was Scott Brosius leading off the top of the seventh with a homer over the left-center-field fence to narrow the lead to 3–1. The forgotten man, Shane Spencer, who replaced Ledee against the lefty, followed with a double to left-center and Bochy rushed to the mound to remove Hitchcock. Joey Hamilton pitched well enough in relief, but the Yankees scored once more in the inning on a passed ball by Leyritz and an error by Caminiti, whose pulled groin was rendering him almost immobile.

The Yankees now trailed by only one run but a well-rested (or was it *too* well rested?) Trevor Hoffman was warming up in the bullpen and was ready to come in as early as the eighth inning. Bochy felt it was necessary when Randy Myers walked O'Neill to open the eighth. "Hell's Bells" blasted over the loudspeakers, but Hoffman could still hear the rousing ovation of the crowd as he walked in from the bullpen like a matador about to dispose of the meanest bull in the arena. So far Hoffman had been erratic in the postseason but there was reason for confidence: The Padres had won fifty-eight consecutive games when he had pitched in a save situation. But it was immediately apparent that Hoffman didn't possess his usual movement or velocity. He was lucky that Bernie Williams's drive died on the warning track for the inning's first out. However, he then walked Martinez, discovering that these Yankees, who would take twenty bases on balls during the four games, were too disciplined to chase anything off the plate. With two men on, Hoffman didn't want to risk walking Brosius, so on a 2-2 count he tried to sneak a fastball by him. But the Yankee third baseman, with Spartan valor, nailed it, powering it over the center-field fence for a three-run homer and a 5–3 Yankee lead. A few minutes before AC/DC had blared through the stadium; now there was stunned silence.

Joe Torre told me that he'd had no idea what kind of player Brosius was when the Yankees acquired him from the A's for a disgruntled Kenny Rogers. He had batted just over .200 in 1997, and it was hoped that injuries had caused the big drop-off in his numbers after a promising 1996 campaign. He wasn't even the Yankees' starting third baseman during spring training. But his fielding impressed Torre and he won the job. He and Derek Jeter would become one of the best left-side infield tandems in baseball, but no one expected him to also drive in ninety-eight runs during the season. And no one expected him to bat .471 in the World Series with two big homers and six RBIs (the same number he had in an equally impressive ALCS). No one expected him to be the World Series MVP and to be the third man on magazine covers with Mark McGwire and Sammy Sosa. "I might have envisioned this," the personable, humble Brosius would say later, "but whether I realistically thought it would happen is another thing. This is the type of thing you dream about as a kid. It's something I've done in my backyard a hundred times. But you never know if you're going to get the opportunity to really do it." Brosius got the opportunity and came through in a big way.

The Padres were able to score a run in the eighth inning off Ramiro Mendoza to narrow the Yankees' lead to 5–4, before Rivera extinguished the low flame. Then, much to their credit, they were able to put on the potential tying and winning runs against Rivera in the ninth inning. As we pointed out during the broadcast, Bochy made a blatant tactical error by having pinch-hitter supreme John Vander Wal pinch-run instead of saving him to do what he does best. Because there is no way that the weak-hitting Andy Sheets should be the batter against Rivera with two outs and the game on the line. It was the ideal situation for Vander Wal, but he wasn't available to hit because he was standing on third base. Rivera struck out Sheets and the Yankees were up 3–0.

As a broadcaster I never like to think that a series is over just because one team is up 3–0. I have seen too many things in baseball to ever count a good team out. Even if they're playing the Yankees. And I was impressed by the Padres fans, who were upbeat when they came to Qualcomm on October 21 for Game 4. Like the players, they had "kept the faith." They had their usual tailgate parties and everybody was as excited about the game as if it were the opening game of the series. Here, too, the fans didn't want the season to end.

With nothing to lose, Bochy gave the ball to Kevin Brown on just three days' rest. He pitched well but gave up a run in the sixth inning and two more in the eighth. How did the Yankees score? In the ugliest ways imaginable. Let's just say that there were a lot of balls bouncing around the infield and, in Scott Brosius's case, dropping in right behind the drawn-in shortstop. And, oh yes, Ricky Ledee twisted the knife in Brown's side again with a sacrifice fly to complete the Yankees' scoring. In his first World Series, the twenty-four-year-old rookie went six-for-ten with four RBIs.

Brown departed after eight innings with a record forty-six strikeouts for the postseason, but it was Andy Pettitte who sparkled by throwing shutout ball for 7⅓ innings and giving up only five hits. Again he awarded Torre for sticking with him despite much outside advice to bypass him in the postseason rotation. Pettitte dedicated his victory to his father, who had just gotten out of the hospital after undergoing a double heart bypass. Until the final day, Andy hadn't been able to join the other players in their celebrations.

The Padres had their best chance to score in the eighth inning, but, as I mentioned elsewhere, Torre brought in Mariano Rivera when Jeff Nelson had a 2-0 count on Caminiti. Nelson was angry at being taken out in the middle of an at-bat, but Torre was wise to do so because he wanted Caminiti to have to hit in this situation against the pitcher who threw the better fastball—Rivera. The Padres' third baseman got a hit but didn't drive the ball out of the ballpark. Rivera prevented any runs from scoring in the eighth inning and preserved the 3–0 shutout in the ninth. In the postseason he gave up 0 runs in 13⅓ innings and batters hit a measly .136 against him. The Yankees could not have had a better closer.

Fittingly, the last ball was hit to Brosius, who scooped up the grounder hit by Mark Sweeney, threw accurately to

Martinez at first, and jumped in the air with joy. Rivera dropped to his knees and shot his arms up to the heavens. And Brosius and the other Yankees piled on in wild celebration.

The Padres looked on without remorse. They had lost all four games yet had shown everyone that they were an excellent and extremely feisty baseball team. "I can't think of one break we had all series," mused Kevin Brown. "They had sixty-hopper, broken-bat hits. It's tough to beat a team with all that talent unless something goes your way. We didn't have a lucky horseshoe, I guess." To beat the Yankees, a team had to get some breaks, but one of the ways the Yankees chose to win was by not giving breaks to opponents.

"I don't know anything we could have done differently and that makes it easier," said Tony Gwynn, who batted .500 for the series. "They played better. It's as simple as that." Gwynn and the other Padres weren't so disheartened by defeat that they forgot the fans. So they returned to the field long after the game ended and had a lovefest with the fans who remained. For both players and fans, it had been a year to remember.

Meanwhile the Yankees had a moving celebration in their clubhouse that saw even George Steinbrenner, of all people, burst into tears over the Yankees' incredible season. If George can cry, you can understand what an effect this season had on baseball fans. It was impossible to be detached.

With the season over, Yankee players at last felt free to make a case that their team deserved consideration as the best ever. It is hard to argue against a team that won 18 of its final 20 games and went 11-2 in the postseason. How can you argue against a team that won 125 games and ended up 75 games over .500 on the seventy-fifth anniversary of the franchise's first world title and the opening of Yankee Stadium? 125 is one of those fan-friendly magical numbers, like 70 and 66, the homer totals of Mark McGwire and Sammy Sosa. What was wonderful about the great and classy Yankee team sweeping the World Series and ending up with that beautifully configured 125-50 record ("That's ridiculous!" exclaimed Derek Jeter about the achievement) was that as a team they provided the excitement and historical contribution that McGwire and Sosa did as individuals. McGwire and Sosa seemed to be an impossible act to follow, but these world-champion Yankees matched them with an incredible performance of their own. For all baseball fans, they provided the perfect conclusion to the perfect season.

About the Authors

TIM MCCARVER is a baseball analyst for the FOX network and for New York Yankee games on WNYW in New York. In a twenty-one-year playing career, he was a star catcher for the Cardinals, Phillies, Expos, and Red Sox. His previous books are *Oh, Baby, I Love It!* and *Baseball for Brain Surgeons and Other Fans,* also written with Danny Peary. He lives in Pennsylvania.

DANNY PEARY has written extensively on television and film, including the books *Cult Movies; Cult Movie Stars;* and *Alternate Oscars.* His sports books include *Cult Baseball Players; We Played the Game: 65 Players Remember Baseball's Greatest Era, 1947–1964;* and *Super Bowl: The Game of Their Lives.* He is the collaborating writer on Tim McCarver's radio show. He lives in New York City.